First edition Ordnance Survey 1:10560 scale map of Edgbaston, surveyed 1882–8; published in 1890.

EDGBASTON
A History

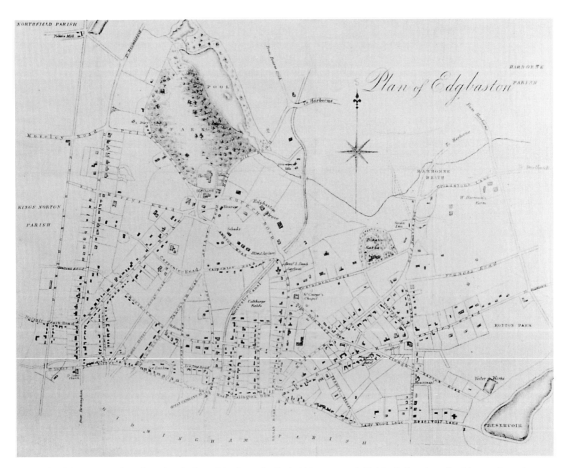

Plan of Edgbaston, 1853: this plan is found in *Price & Co.'s Directory and Guide*, it is printed with south at the top so it may be easier to read upside down!

EDGBASTON
A History

with best wishes

Terry Slater

Terry R. Slater

Phillimore

2002

Published by
PHILLIMORE & CO. LTD
Shopwyke Manor Barn, Chichester, West Sussex

ISBN 1 86077 216 1

Printed and bound in Great Britain by
BIDDLES LTD
Guildford, Surrey

Contents

To Keith and Mary Ford,
with thanks for thirty years of friendship

List of Illustrations

Frontispiece: Plan of Edgbaston, 1853

Preface and Acknowledgements

There has never been a reasonably comprehensive history of Edgbaston, perhaps because it is one of those non-places—a suburb. But what a suburb! Until about 1800 it was an out-of-the-way place of little consequence. Then, for a century, it became the 'Belgravia of Birmingham', the place where the city's industrial and commercial élite lived in splendid isolation from mere mortals because of the close control of development by the Calthorpe family, who owned four-fifths of the parish. It was a treasure trove of English domestic 19th-century architecture. Through the 20th century much of the remaining rural land and many of the largest houses were given over to institutions of one kind or another, but especially to educational and health-related institutions. Today, it remains a remarkable suburb by any standards. Given its élite status, its history in the 19th century is the history of the wider city, since almost everyone of any significance lived in Edgbaston. In a book of this kind, their stories have had to be limited to brief glimpses when they impinge more directly on the Edgbaston scene. For some tastes, buildings and institutions will be seen to loom too large in the story of Edgbaston presented here, but this reflects my own particular interests and I make no apology for it.

Any book of this kind is dependent on the research and writing of others and I am especially grateful for the volumes published on the development of the Calthorpe estate by Professor David Cannadine; on the history of the University of Birmingham by Professor Eric Ives and his co-authors; on the garden history of Edgbaston by Phillida Ballard, and on cricket by Leslie Duckworth. I am grateful to the staff of the Local Studies Department of Birmingham City Library, and of the Archives Department, for their assistance with bibliographical and photographic researches, especially Paul Taylor, the photography officer. Victoria Emmanuel showed me the collection of local prints and drawings in the Birmingham Museum and Art Gallery, and Catherine Clark helped by providing photographs from the Winterbourne Gardens collection.

The staff of the University of Birmingham Library, its Special Collections, and the Barber Institute Library, have been unfailingly helpful in aiding my researches. Toni Demidowicz of the conservation section of Birmingham City Council's Department of Planning and Architecture enabled me to see the unpublished survey of Edgbaston's historic gardens and the Conservation Area report. My colleagues Michael Tanner and John Bryson were helpful, in obtaining information on Priory Tennis Club and in providing copies of earlier university publications, respectively. Joe Heaton helped me with information on Edgbaston Old Church and Rev. Simon Thorburn enabled me to see the historical material in St George's Church. My graduate student Christopher James, former head teacher of Harborne Hill School, has been a mine of information on the schools of Edgbaston and some of its institutions, for which I am especially grateful. He persuaded Sister Hilary to provide photographs of St Paul's School from their archives. My friends David Barge, Alan Duxbury, Keith Ford, Daryll Holloway and Liz Veal helped find illustrations and information. I owe a particular debt of gratitude to my technical colleagues in the School of Geography and Environmental Sciences at the University of Birmingham: to Jamie Peart for providing maps and volumes from our Birmingham Collection; to Ann Ankcorn for drawing the original maps and, most especially, to Geoff Dowling ARPS for photographic services above and beyond the call of duty.

I have worked in Edgbaston for 30 years looking out on the landscapes of the university, and for 15 of those years helped run the 74th Birmingham Scout Group (St Germains) in Portland Road. That is how I got to know Keith and Mary Ford. Keith was Group Scout Leader and has been a member of the Group since he was eight. His reminiscences of growing up in north Edgbaston, and of his career in the West Midlands Fire Service, and Mary's hospitality every Friday night, have helped keep academic feet on the ground. They have allowed me the privilege of sharing the many joys and occasional sorrows of their family's life and have shared mine in return. I could have no better friends and this book is for them.

Illustration Acknowledgements

Illustrations are reproduced by the kind permission of the following: Birmingham City Library, frontispiece, 3, 4, 13, 24, 43, 44, 51-53, 55, 56, 66, 68, 76, 80, 82, 93, 94, 97, 98, 100-2, 109, 128, 130, 131, 138, 139, 140, 144, 151, 153; The University of Birmingham, 105-7, 110-12, 114-7, 123, 125, 133; University of Birmingham, School of Geography and Environmental Sciences, 27, 32, 48, 92, 148, 154; Winterbourne Botanical Garden, 59-61; St Paul's School, 136, 137; King Edward's School, 132, 134; Phillimore & Co., 7; St Germain's Scout Group, 86; Mrs W. Barge, 74; Mr G. Dowling ARPS, 12, 34, 129, 152; Dr T.R. Slater, 1, 11, 14, 16, 19, 26, 28, 29, 31, 33, 35-40, 42, 47, 49, 63, 64, 81, 88, 96, 99, 113, 118-20, 124, 126, 141, 142, 145, 146, 149, 156-8, 161, 162, 165; Mr A.H. Spettigue, 58; Mrs L. Veal, 22, 79, 83-5; Airviews(M/cr) Ltd. Manchester Airport, 41.

One

Roman Edgbaston

The Land

For most of its history Edgbaston has been a rather remote place and a very small place. It stands high on the Birmingham plateau and encloses the ridge between the valleys of the rivers Tame and Rea and their small tributary streams. Along the ridge, where Hagley Road now runs, was a routeway as old as almost any in England, part of a long-distance trading route between the Welsh border and central England where the stone to make polished axe-heads was brought from Wales. Only a little of Edgbaston's lands looked northwards to the Tame, and most of that was woodland or heath through to the medieval period. This was because the soils on the ridge top were stony and sandy since they were derived from the deposits of the great glaciers of the Ice Age.

Most of the land was to the south of the ridge top, sloping gently down towards the valley of the Bourn Brook, which formed the southern boundary of the land unit. Through the centre was another even smaller stream, the Chad Brook, which joined the Bourn Brook just before that stream itself joined the River Rea on its journey on to where Birmingham was to develop. These streams and rivers were small, but fast-flowing, and after prolonged heavy rain they would swell rapidly and often flooded the meadows on either side. They were to make good mill sites in later times. The rather larger pebbles in the river beds were used by prehistoric peoples to create what archaeologists have called 'burnt mounds', great

circular heaps of stones with a depression in the middle, the stones showing evidence of being heated in a fire. The usual explanation of these enigmatic remains is that they were an early type of sauna. A fire would be lit in a skin-covered timber frame; large pebbles would be heated in the fire and then dropped into water to create steam. Burnt mounds characterise all Birmingham's river valleys. The northern side on the Bourn Brook valley is marked by a rather steeper slope, where a geological fault in the underlying Mercian Mudstones (soft, reddish sandstones) has influenced the topography. The fault also brings

1   The Chad Brook: from Richmond Hill Road the Chad Brook looks like a country stream.

more and less permeable rocks together so that large numbers of springs are thrown out along the bottom of the slope; even today they can still be observed flowing across the pavements beside the Bristol Road in wet periods.

Metchley Fort

In Roman times Edgbaston was the most important place in the Birmingham region. From around A.D. 48, for at least the next 150 years, a large fortress occupied the hilltop at Metchley, where the university medical school now stands. It is a good defensive site on a nearly level spur of land at about 450 feet OD with quite steep slopes on three sides. Only to the north-west does the land rise slightly. It was located where three Roman roads met. The most important was probably Ryknield Street which left the Fosse Way near Bourton-on-the-Water, crossed the Avon valley at Bidford, went through the small Roman industrial town at Alcester and, having crossed Weatheroak Hill near Wythall, proceeded to the south entrance of the fort.

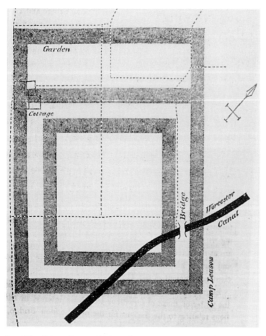

2 Finch's plan of the forts in 1822: John Finch published his description of Metchley in the *Quarterly Journal of Science, Literature and the Arts.*

North of the fort, the road continued to be called Ryknield Street in medieval times, passing to the north of Birmingham, through the western side of Sutton Park (where a length of the road has been preserved/reconstructed) and on to the small Roman town at Wall, on Watling Street. The third, more elusive, road came from Droitwich via Bromsgrove, approaching Metchley from the south-west.

The fort is noticed by William Hutton in his *History of Birmingham* (1783) but he ascribed it to 'those pilfering vermin the Danes'! John Finch published a description and plan in 1822 and both authors note that pieces of swords and axes were ploughed up from the fields within the bounds of the fort. The Birmingham and Worcester Canal cut through the south-east quadrant of the fort in a deep cutting, but seemingly the excavators found nothing. The railway followed the same line in the later 19th century, and the Elan Valley aqueduct crossed the site soon after. However, it was not until the construction of the Queen Elizabeth Hospital and Medical School in the 1930s that some archaeological excavations at last took place. As more and more of the fort has been destroyed by the expansion of the university in the later 20th century, further archaeological excavations have been carried out and tell us quite a lot about the history of the fort.

The earliest fort was of square plan with sides of roughly 220 yards. The defences consisted of an earthen rampart, about 18 feet wide, covered with turf, with two 'v'-shaped ditches outside dug into the subsoil, each about 15 feet wide and 6 feet deep. There would have been a timber palisade on the rampart, timber gateways in the middle of each side, and corner guard towers. That in the north-west corner was excavated in 1954 when a reconstruction of the defences was being prepared for public display. In the north-west corner, two timber barrack blocks for the soldiers have been excavated and suggest a date in the Claudian period (A.D. 41-54) for the construction of this first fort. The northernmost block was a double

3 Excavations at Metchley in 1968: archaeologists began excavating at Metchley in the 1930s.

4 The reconstructed corner tower: a corner tower was excavated in 1954 and partly reconstructed to show the public what it might have looked like.

block built back-to-back to save space and timber. The rooms were arranged in rows of four, each room accommodating four men. It is thought that this was the accommodation of four cavalry units, each comprising 32 men. Corridors separated the men's rooms from further rooms at the ends of these barrack blocks which might have formed the officer's quarters. Other buildings excavated from this first phase included a granary, workshop and stores building.

All these buildings would have been carefully constructed within the regular grid of gravelled roads that divided the interior of the fort in the manner prescribed in military regulations. Part of the road inside the defences was excavated in 1954 and proved to be made of several inches thickness of tightly packed gravel.

Enormous quantities of constructional timber were needed, which was usually cut, sawn and prepared on site. In total about a thousand men would have garrisoned the fort and it would not have been long before local people began to gather near the gates of such a military establishment. Soldiers usually had money to spend on such things as additional food and drink, trinkets, little luxuries that made barrack life easier, and sex. At Metchley, we know that such an irregular settlement of traders and camp followers, under military supervision, began to develop at the west gate of the fort in this earliest phase.

Sometime in the mid- or later first century the fort was extended to the north, east and south by annexes, which were also defended

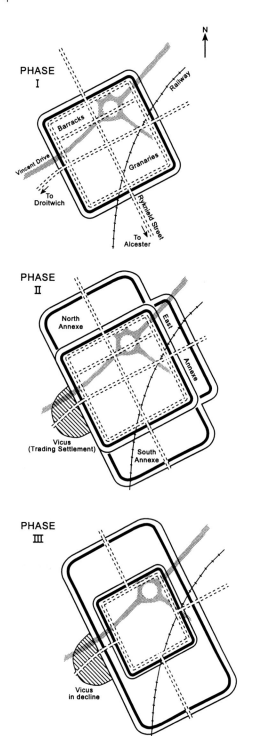

PHASE
I

PHASE
II

PHASE
III

5 Metchley Roman forts: this sequence of plans shows
how the fort was reconstructed at least three times over
perhaps seventy years.

with rampart and double ditches. There were
no buildings in these annexes, however, and
the archaeologists suggest that they may have
been used for open-air storage of non-perishable
goods and for tethering the horses of the cavalry.
At the same time some of the buildings were
remodelled internally to provide extra storage
space. This suggests that the garrison was
reduced in size as the military frontier moved
west and north and Metchley became an
important stores supply depot.

Later still in the first century the barrack
blocks and stores buildings were dismantled and
removed, but the defences continued to be fully
maintained and manned. A new series of
buildings replaced the barracks but they were
laid out very irregularly. They mostly comprised
small timber and wattle buildings in compounds.
Some seem to have been used for livestock and
stabling, others were hearths and ovens, yet
others were for iron-working. By this phase of
occupation it may be that the fort had been
reduced to an extended period of 'care-taking'
and a well-behind-the-lines stores depot.

Towards the end of the first century active
soldiers returned to the site and a new, smaller,
fort was constructed within the defences of the
first one. This, too, had a turf-revetted rampart
and exterior ditch and, at the same time, the
older ditches were recut to make a formidable
series of defences. Unfortunately, the rampart
seems not to have been constructed very well as
it was quickly replaced with another with timber
strengthening. Inside this new fort the only
buildings found were granaries and a cook-house,
which has led the excavators to suggest that the
garrison accommodation might have been in
tents. Finally, dating from the second century,
more ditches have been found in the south-east
corner, suggesting that the fort was still in use
for one activity or another. One possibility, given
its strategic location on the road network, was
that there was a *mansio*, or inn, here, for the
accommodation of official messengers and
stabling for their horses; though no specific
buildings of this kind have been found.

Two

Medieval Edgbaston

There are no early medieval references to Edgbaston and so we must infer what was happening in the area from indirect evidence. To do this we need to broaden the scope of our enquiries somewhat so that we can see Edgbaston's relationships with its neighbours and try to discover how people, settlement, farming, and the church were evolving between the fifth and the 11th centuries. The first thing to observe is that Edgbaston is at the edge, on the borders of events, not at the heart. The Birmingham plateau was not good farming country and therefore it was well-wooded, pastoral countryside with heathland on the sandier, pebbly soils; there were scattered farmsteads and no hint of a nucleated village settlement. This was so into modern times and it was certainly so in the early medieval period. In the early post-Roman years population probably fell, as it did elsewhere, but certainly not to the extent that farming ceased. Edgbaston should certainly not be thought of as a woodland and heathland waste waiting for the Anglo-Saxons to arrive and repopulate it.

As Anglo-Saxon peoples slowly migrated into this region from the Trent and Avon valleys to live amongst the Romano-British, perhaps only in the sixth century in this part of the west midlands, it was their language that supplanted that of the longer-established British and gave name to places. Edgbaston derives from a farmer's personal name, *Ecgbeald*, and means Ecgbeald's farm, which was perhaps located where Edgbaston Hall was later to stand. Some surrounding places have names which suggest earlier groups of settlers. Harborne, for example, to the west, is a 'topographical' name—it means 'muddy stream', and place-name scholars usually reckon this type of name amongst the earliest in Anglo-Saxon naming practices. Perhaps only slightly later are *-inga-* names, which mean 'the people of—', indicative of a group of settlers under a leader. Neighbouring Birmingham is of this kind and means 'the settlement of the people of a man called *Beorma*'. Northwards from Edgbaston were later *-tun* and *-wic* names which, like Edgbaston, perhaps date from the eighth or ninth centuries: places such as Smethwick, the farm of the smiths; West Bromwich, the farm in the district where broom grows; and Rotton, the cheerful farm; whilst to the south was Selly, one of a group of '-ley' names, meaning 'wood' or 'woodland clearing' (Bartley, Frankley, Weoley and Moseley are the others) which ring the open field land implied by Northfield's name. Weoley is the most interesting of the '-ley' names as it implies the presence of a pagan place of worship in a wood or woodland clearing (*weoh* means idol). There are other such pagan names to the north at Wednesfield and Wednesbury where the worship of Woden is implied.

By the seventh century a new administrative geography was beginning to emerge and this gives us some more clues to the nature of early-medieval Edgbaston. To begin with, Christian dioceses were created to reflect the tribal groupings of the Anglo-Saxons. To the

6 Ancient parish boundaries: the complex arrangement of Edgbaston's ecclesiastical and civil boundaries is shown on this plan.

north Lichfield served the Mercians, whilst to the south Worcester served the Hwiccians. The boundary between the two dioceses ran along the Bourn Brook, the southern boundary of Harborne and Edgbaston, as far as Balsall Heath where it went over the watershed to the Cole valley and on south. Edgbaston belonged to Lichfield, and therefore to the Mercian Trent-valley kingdom, or at least it did when this boundary is first described much later on, in the 13th century. Edgbaston was therefore not only marginal farming land; it was also marginal politically, on the borders of two kingdoms. Evidence suggests that at both Lichfield and Worcester there were surviving Romano-British Christian communities who were using the still-surviving churches of St Michael's and St Helen's respectively for worship. That is probably why bishops were located there. Pastorally, the early medieval church operated through minsters, churches with a number of priests who went out preaching, pastoring and evangelising over a very wide parochial territory. By the eighth century more minsters were being founded as the Christian community grew, especially in the outer limits of the oldest minster parishes. It seems likely that St Peter's Church at Harborne and SS Peter and Paul's Church at Aston were minsters of this period. Edgbaston was part of Harborne's minster parish, as was Smethwick, West Bromwich and Handsworth, and possibly Birmingham too.

More detailed secular administrative patterns do not become clear until the shire system of the late 10th or early 11th centuries. Once more Edgbaston found itself on a boundary and, surprisingly, it was separated from its church at Harborne. Harborne, Smethwick, West Bromwich and Handsworth were placed in Staffordshire and administered from the *burh* at Stafford built in 904 by Aethelflaeda, Lady of the Mercians. South of the Bourn Brook, Northfield, Selly, and Kings Norton looked to Worcestershire, which encompassed most of the former Hwiccan territory (Hwicce had by then been incorporated into greater Mercia). To the south-east another shire was created centred on an earlier trading centre at Warwick, which, like Stafford and Tamworth, had been fortified by Aethelflaeda in the early 10th century. Edgbaston and Birmingham were allocated to Warwickshire, finding themselves almost surrounded by the lands of other shires. Their local hundred court was at Coleshill, another of the early minster parish centres of this region.

Domesday Edgbaston

Following the Norman Conquest, Domesday Book gives us a little more information about the manor of Edgbaston in 1086. It had been granted to William, son of Ansculf, together with most of the surrounding manors in Warwickshire and Staffordshire, including Birmingham. This huge estate was later to evolve into the honour of the earls of Dudley. William sub-let his lands to lesser lords, in Edgbaston's case to a man called Drogo. Before 1066, Domesday tells us that Edgbaston's lands had been held freely by two men, Aski and Alfwy. It was a modest estate with a tax liability of only two hides.

The Domesday commissioners were told that there was arable land for four ploughs, but they record that the lord had one and a half ploughs and the farmers had another five ploughs. Where ploughs exceed ploughland, as in Edgbaston, it suggests numbers of fairly small farms, most with some arable land. These farms were quite prosperous, however, since many of the farmers could afford their own plough and plough team of oxen, rather than sharing with their neighbours. There was some sharing though, since there were ten farmers sharing

five ploughs. Neighbouring Birmingham was exactly the opposite. There were six ploughlands of arable but only three ploughs, two of them shared between nine farmers, suggesting that Birmingham's farmers were poorer and not using all their arable land. The tax value suggests that the prosperity in Edgbaston was recent since its worth had increased 50 per cent between 1066 and 1086, from 20 shillings to 30 shillings. This was probably because farmers were being encouraged to bring new lands into cultivation in the manor. Seven of Edgbaston's 10 farmers were bordars, who usually held their land for money rents after bringing it into cultivation from heath or woodland. The other three were villeins, who held their land in exchange for working on the lord's land for some of each week, or at ploughing or harvest time. Finally, Domesday tells us that there was a wood half a league long and three furlongs wide (1500 paces or one and a half miles by 660 yards). The early 18th-century estate maps of Edgbaston suggest that this woodland was in the far north-west of the parish on the northern slopes of the valley of the Chad Brook, since this area was still woodland then. The earlier of the two maps also suggests that the manor's common arable land was around the later site of Edgbaston Hall, since here there were a number of very large fields which may once have been ploughed in open-field strips. By 1701, the largest of these, more than 50 acres in extent, was called the 'great cowpaster' but the conversion of arable into pasture was a common feature of the 16th and 17th centuries.

De. W. ten Drogo. ii. hid in CELBOLDESTONE. Tra. ē
iiii. car. In dnio. ē. i. car 7 dim. 7 iii. uilli 7 vii. bord
cū. v. car. Silua. iii. qrent lat. 7 dim leuu lg.
Valuit. xx. sol. Modo. xxx. Aschi 7 Aluui libe tenuer.

7 Edgbaston's Domesday record: Domesday Book provides a concise record of land-holding and agriculture.

Just as important to our appreciation of the manor are the negatives in Domesday Book: there was no priest or church, since Edgbaston was still part of St Peter's Harborne parish, despite the fact that the manor had been in a different shire for a century or more. More surprising is that there is no mention of a mill, or of meadowland attached to the manor, although the valleys of the Chad, Bourn Brook and Rea abut or run through the manor. Such things were valuable attributes and are usually mentioned in Domesday if they were present in 1086. Finally, there is no mention of the great park at Metchley. Parks are only infrequently mentioned in Domesday, mainly because it was the Normans themselves who were the makers of these distinctive enclosures in the countryside used for hunting deer. Metchley may have been enclosed after 1086 therefore, but its name derives from the Old English for 'great enclosure' (*micel gehæg*) suggesting that it originates before the 11th century, though it could be argued that the name refers to the earthworks of the Roman fortress in the middle of a later park.

Later Medieval Edgbaston

In the 1230s Edgbaston was still within the Barony of Dudley, now held by the de Somery family, but on the death of Roger de Somery in 1235 his inquisition post mortem shows that the local lord was William de Birmingham. Edgbaston was already firmly tied with the growing prosperity of its neighbour therefore. In 1166 William's father, Peter de Birmingham, had purchased the right from the Crown to hold a weekly market at Birmingham, beside his 'castle'. In the following half century the market had prospered and new tenants had been attracted to the place so that Birmingham had become a flourishing small town. William, when he succeeded to the estate in 1189, sensibly confirmed his father's market charter with the king, but this time Birmingham is described as a 'villa' or town. One of the reasons that Birmingham developed so rapidly is that its

lords did not seek to found a borough, with all the expense of another charter, but simply granted burgage tenure (the right to hold and transfer land freely for a fixed annual rent and to trade in the market) to all who came to live and work there. Still more important was the fact that the rent for a plot of land was only 8d. a year, rather than the usual 12d., and the fact that Birmingham was the first market founded in this northern part of the shire. It was no doubt the profits from this town-founding activity that enabled the de Birminghams to become lords of neighbouring Edgbaston too.

The de Birminghams did not farm the lands of Edgbaston themselves, but sub-let to another family who like their lords took their name from their manor so, for much of the 13th and early 14th centuries, it was the de Edgbaston family who lived on the hilltop where the hall still stands. It was Henry de Edgbaston, sometime in the early 1270s, who was responsible for building a chapel beside his manor house which was dedicated to St Bartholomew. Soon afterwards, in 1279, the little chapel was plunged into controversy when the incumbent of Harborne, Canon Henry de Ganio, claimed the living of Harborne church and its chapel at Edgbaston as his own. After adjudication, he surrendered it to the Bishop of Coventry and Lichfield in exchange for an annual payment of 30 marks (£20) to be paid during de Ganio's lifetime. The bishop, in turn, gave it to the Dean and Chapter of Lichfield Cathedral, who had claimed it as theirs in the first place. In 1287 Henry de Edgbaston claimed that, as the builder of the chapel of Edgbaston, he had the right to present a priest to serve there, but the Dean and Chapter prevailed on him, in exchange for the similar very large sum of £20, to agree that they had the right of presentation. It was to remain with the Dean and Chapter through to about 1725, when it was obtained by Sir Richard Gough when he substantially augmented the living.

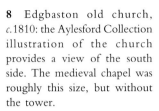

8 Edgbaston old church, *c.*1810: the Aylesford Collection illustration of the church provides a view of the south side. The medieval chapel was roughly this size, but without the tower.

These legal disputes are recorded in the Great Register Book of Lichfield, which also records several property transactions in Edgbaston. The most interesting of these is the transfer of a plot of land from John FitzWilliam Porter to St Peter's, Harborne. He had earlier acquired this from Henry de Edgbaston, who reserved to himself the burial ground and Jewry. Since late-medieval Jewish communities in England are almost exclusively urban in character, it may be that several Jewish families were operating as merchants or money-lenders in Birmingham. In 1290 all Jews were expelled from the kingdom by Edward I. We can also note that the Porter family were still farming land in Edgbaston in the 18th century.

Sometime in the 13th century the de Birminghams decided to enclose the heathlands and poor farmland to the north of the Hagley Road ridgeway into a park. Parks were a fashionable attribute for any well-to-do family in the 13th and 14th centuries and their main purpose was as a fenced enclosure for deer. They were normally surrounded by a bank with an internal ditch, and with an oak pale fence about six feet high on the top of the bank, which effectively prevented the deer leaping out. Venison was an important part of the winter diet for land-owning families, whilst also enabling them to enjoy the pleasures of hunting over their lands. It was as well to get the permission of the king before enclosing a deer park because deer-hunting was otherwise reserved to the king. Rotton Park, as it became known, was about 600 acres in size and was mostly beyond the bounds of Edgbaston, in Birmingham parish. Though not as large as the Earl of Warwick's great park at Wedgnock, Rotton Park was certainly amongst the larger deer parks in Warwickshire.

We first hear of it in 1307, when Walter de Stafford, John, son of Thomas Grynoe, and Alexander de Turberville were indicted at Warwick Assizes for poaching in the 'Parc de Rotton juxta Birmingham'. Poaching was always a problem for the owners of deer parks and poachers were as likely to be neighbouring landowners enjoying some illegal sport, as in this case, as they were tenant farmers or out-laws. To try to deter poachers and to look after the deer there was usually a park keeper living in a lodge within the bounds of the park. There was such a lodge in Rotton Park on the site of the later Rotton Park Farm, which survived to the late 19th century. There were other people living within the bounds, too, since an

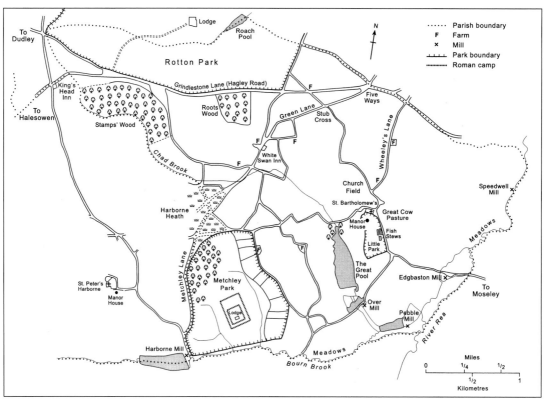

9 Later medieval Edgbaston: the landscape of later medieval Edgbaston can be partly reconstructed from maps and documents.

inquisition in 1425 noted that there were 10 cottages in the park. Since parks were so strongly enclosed, in a generally open country-side, they were also useful for other things. They often contained separate enclosures for the lord's horses and many parks contained ponds for the breeding of fish, another impor-tant part of the medieval diet. Rotton Park was no exception and the pond, later known as Roach Pool, which was where Rotton Park Reservoir now is, was described in a survey of the manor of Birmingham in 1529: 'ther ys a perke belongynge to the same manor wherein ys a greate ponde which ys overgrowen wt wedes and rede and lytell fyshe ar now therin and the logge ys sore decayed'. Clearly, the park was not being well maintained and soon after, in 1553, the park was disparked and divided up into pasture closes.

Edgbaston's other deer park was the rather smaller one at Metchley, and this also belonged to the de Birminghams through much of the medieval period. However, we know far less about Metchley than we do about Rotton. The one thing we are sure about is its bounds, since it appears on the 1701 and 1718 estate plans of Edgbaston, whereas the boundaries of Rotton are largely conjectural. Metchley's boundary is shown as still surrounded by a pale fence and about a quarter of its area is taken up by wood-land. It, too, had a lodge, located in the central enclosure provided by the banks of the Roman fortification, and, by 1701, much of its south-eastern and south-western edges consisted of enclosed fields which, together with the open area of the park, were being farmed by Richard Reeve. These fields may represent horse pastures from the medieval period.

We get to know a little of some of Edgbaston's principal families in the 14th century from the national tax returns known as the Lay Subsidies levied in 1327 and 1332 (see Table 1 on page 12). The first thing to notice is that a very high proportion of the farmers and others on whom tax was levied in 1332 were named William: 11 out of 19! Some of the names are the same in 1327 of course, when there were eight Williams. Some names tell us about occupations: a walker, a porter, a carter, a smith; others tell us where people lived: in the 'hay' (almost certainly Metchley Park), by the Ryefield, at 'Scholle', on the hill (Hulle); and some tell us where people came from: from Hinkley (Leicestershire), from Tickenhill, and from Coughton. Normally it is possible to get another snapshot of late medieval population from the late 14th-century Poll Tax returns, but the Warwickshire returns, and especially those for Hemlingford Hundred in which Edgbaston was situated, have been badly damaged and are illegible.

Lords of the Manor

The de Edgbaston family continued to hold Edgbaston manor from the de Birminghams for more than a century. During this time they held fiscal and military administrative positions in the shire whereby they acted as assessors and collectors of the Lay Subsidy. On another occasion they were responsible for assembling 600 foot soldiers from Warwickshire and Leicestershire to join Edward II's army against the Scots. In the late 14th century the last of the male line, Richard, died leaving his daughter Isabella as his heiress. Isabella was married to Thomas Middlemore, a London merchant whose ancestral home was in Mappleborough Green in Studley parish. As part of the marriage settlement he became lord of Edgbaston. The Middlemores were destined to remain resident in Edgbaston's manor house until the later 17th century. Thomas's younger son, Nicholas, married another heiress, Agnes Hawkeslowe, who owned the estate of Hawkesley in Kings Norton parish, so there were two dynasties of

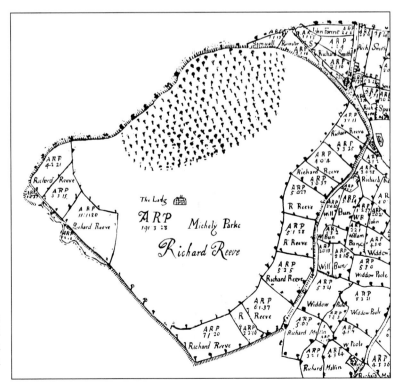

10 Metchley Park: Metchley's fenced boundary was still maintained when William Deeley came to draw his plan in 1701.

1327 Lay Subsidy		1332 Lay Subsidy	
Names	Tax Paid	Names	Tax Paid
Elena Hinkeleye	3s.	John, Lord of Edgbaston	3s.
Rado de Hinkleye	6d.		
Wilo de Tykenhull	2s. 6d.	Adam de Tykenhull	1s. 8d.
Nicho de Tykenhull	1s. 6d.	Nicholas de Tykenhull	2s. 6d.
Wilo le Walkar	2s.	Richard le Walker	2s.
Wilo le Porter	2s.	William le Porter	2s.
Wilo Jonns	12d.	William Jones	1s. 8d.
Wilo en le Hay	12d.	William, son of Robert in Hay	12d.
Julean atte Scholle	12d.	Juliana atte Scholle	2s. 6d.
Henr. atte Scholle	1s. 6d.		
Willo fil Thome	10d.	William Tommen	1s. 8d.
Wilo de Ruyfeld	12d.	William de Ruyfeld	2s.
Thom Perys	12d.	Thomas Person	12d.
Johne atte felde	12d.	John de Cofton	12d.
Rico de Tokkeleye	12d.	William atte Nassh	2s.
Wilo son of Rogi	12d.	William Judden	2s.
Robto Waleys	12d.	William Nicken	2s.
John fabr. (smith)	10d.	William Osbarn	1s. 6d.
Nicho ate Hulle	10d.	William Hanecokes	1s. 6d.
		James Tropynel	1s. 6d.
		William le Carter	12d.
Total	24s. 6d.		33s. 6d.

Table 1. The 1327 and 1332 Lay Subsidies

Middlemores living to the south-west of Birmingham. Though the London cloth trade probably provided the larger part of Thomas Middlemore's income, he did not neglect his local market town since he was amongst the benefactors of the guild of the Holy Cross in Birmingham, endowing them with lands in Edgbaston. In 1396 we know from an inquisition that his Edgbaston manor was providing him with £41 6s. 8d. in rents. He died in 1409, Isabella having borne him six children. One of the daughters, Joyce, became prioress of the small convent of Henwood, in Knowle parish.

Isabella remarried and continued to live at the Edgbaston manor house until her death in 1423, as did her second husband Richard Clodshale of Saltley, until his death five years

later. Only then could John Middlemore, eldest son of Thomas and Isabella, take possession of the manor. John died in 1466-7 whilst his son, Richard, was still a minor, so the estate was administered for a period by Sir William Birmingham, his feudal lord. Richard married Margery Throckmorton from Coughton Court and they had two sons. Richard died in 1503 and we know from his will that he was buried in Edgbaston churchyard. He gave 5d. each to the churches of Edgbaston and Lichfield, and to the guilds of Birmingham and Deritend. Margery, rather than remarry, took a solemn vow of chastity before the bishop and thereafter wore the cloak and veil of widowhood for nearly thirty years. When she died her will directed 'John Baker my preest to sing in the church of Eggebaston a hole year'.

Three

Reformation and the Civil War

In the troubled years of the Reformation both the Middlemore families of Hawkesley and of Edgbaston remained true to Roman Catholicism and hence appear on the rolls compiled in troubled times as recusants. A number of the family became priests, probably including Blessed Humphrey Middlemore, a Carthusian monk who was proctor of the London Charterhouse and who was executed with others of his fraternity in 1535. These martyrs were beatified by the pope in 1886. Humphrey is thought to be a younger son of Margery Throckmorton (another prominent Roman Catholic family, who still live at Coughton Court, Warwickshire) and Richard Middlemore. Despite their Catholicism in the Reformation period, the Middlemore family continued to play a significant part in county affairs. Richard and Margery's grandson, Robert, for example, who inherited the estate, was to become Sheriff of Warwickshire in 1567-8, despite the fact that two years later he refused to sign the articles which provided for the new Book of Common Prayer to be used in parish churches, as did the Throckmortons. Robert's younger brother, meanwhile, was Rector of Birmingham from 1536 until 1554. Robert's eldest son, Richard (II), seems to have been a rather unpleasant character who several times was brought to court in the Star Chamber for beating tenants or neighbours who did not do as he wished. Though a registered recusant, he was not disloyal to the Crown since he is known to have subscribed the substantial sum of £25

to the fund for the defence of the kingdom against the Spanish Armada in 1587. He and his wife Anne had at least 11 children.

Whatever the character of Richard Middlemore, his eldest son, Robert (II), was sent off to Oxford University in 1574; he may also have gone to the English College in Rome for further studies. Despite this he was not registered as a recusant, and possibly disguised his Catholicism. His second son, Humphrey, was certainly a Catholic since he too went to the English College, and was ordained priest in Rome in 1619. The eldest son, Richard (III), who succeeded to the Edgbaston estate in 1633-4, was trained as a lawyer and was admitted to Staple Inn of the Middle Temple in 1607. He was 'a delinquent and a papist' and had to lease his lands back from the Crown at a fee of £100 per year so that his legal skills were much needed in a series of complex property deals which saw many of the farms leased to the Porter family. A letter survives which he wrote to the astrologer, Robert Napier, describing the untoward events of 'great stormes of lightning, thunder, hail and raine', probably in Metchley Park: '3 men standing under a tree under which they had droven a teame of six oxen laden with hay to avoid the violence of the storme, the men were all stroaken suddenly to the ground but one of them recovered life again, and 3 of the Oxen … were also stroaken stark dead'. In the last years of his life the Civil War had broken out and Edgbaston Hall was clearly a target for Parliamentary troops.

11 The *White Swan* inn, Harborne Road probably dates from the 17th century.

Civil War

In 1644 Edgbaston Hall fell into the hands of Colonel John Fox of Walsall, known to his enemies as 'Tinker' Fox in reference to his previous trade. He gathered together 16 of his 'swete brethren' and marched on Edgbaston Hall. He fortified the house using timber from the church roof and garrisoned it eventually with some 200 troops including cavalry, whose horses were stabled in the church. In order to provide for his troops the surrounding countryside was ravaged of food and horses. In June Parliament officially ordered Fox to 'hold the mansion-house and manor of Edgbaston', and to receive the revenues payable to Middlemore. Middlemore meanwhile was with the king's garrison at Worcester and helped besiege his kinsman's house at Hawkesley. It is said that he offered the Royalist troops there a large sum of money if they would go and besiege Fox at Edgbaston Hall. He died in 1647 and had to be buried at Studley.

His eldest son, Robert (III), survived him by only five years, dying aged 28. His two young children, Richard (IV) and Mary, were sent to Sir Edward Nichols, Bt of Faxton, Northamptonshire by Parliament 'in trust to breed them up Protestants'. Sir Edward failed, because Mary was baptised in the Catholic chapel in Birmingham in 1671 and married another Catholic, Sir John Gage, Bt. Richard Middlemore died young in 1660-1, the last male heir of the family. The mistreated Edgbaston Hall was certainly a very large house since it was taxed for 27 hearths in 1663, but it was not to stand for much longer since, at the Glorious Revolution in 1688, the mob from Birmingham surged out from the town and burnt it to the ground, 'fearing it might be made a place of sanctuary and resort for the papists'.

A Franciscan priest, Leo Randolph, had been working in Birmingham since 1657. In 1687 a small cruciform chapel, dedicated to St Mary Magdalene, was built in Masshouse Lane, for which Sir John Gage subscribed £190, but it was burnt the following year by the same mob who destroyed Edgbaston Hall. Randolph therefore moved out from the town and began saying mass in a farmhouse on the Edgbaston estate, which still survives as Masshouse Farm in Pritchatts Road. A school was added from

12   Masshouse Farm, Pritchatts Road, built *c*.1680. The windows on the right are painted onto plaster. They were filled in to avoid the window tax in the 18th century.

1725. In the late 17th century Edgbaston was the most Catholic parish in the district and it was only in the later 18th century that Birmingham Catholic residents began to out-number those from Edgbaston. The Franciscan mission left Edgbaston in 1786, when St Peter's Chapel was built in Broad Street.

Mills

By the 16th century there were four mills in Edgbaston. The oldest was presumably Edgbaston Mill, which stood beside the River Rea, where the lane to Moseley crossed the river (opposite today's County Cricket Ground). It is first documented in the 13th century, in 1284, when it was burgled! In the 18th century it was examined by James Watt, who reported that it had four sets of millstones and an over-shot wheel 8 feet wide and 7 ft. 6 in. in diameter. Further down the Rea was Speedwell Mill, whilst upstream, on the Bourn Brook, was Pebble Mill, and just above that, on the Chad Brook, was Over Mill. These last two were used for cloth by the 16th century, since the will of John Kynge in 1557 gave his son Roger 'one fullyng myll in Edgbaston' with 'liberty to

occupy and cullor clothe in my dyyinge house'. The water from the Chad and Bourn Brooks was insufficient to power the mills in the summer months and so both had mill ponds. Over Mill ultimately had the benefit of two ponds. Its main pool was Spurrier's Pool fed by the springs from the Birmingham fault but, since the huge lake in Edgbaston Park was constructed well before the landscaping of the park, its principal intention must have been to improve the water supply for the mill.

In the 17th century Over Mill, Pebble Mill and Speedwell Mill were blade mills used for sharpening edge tools such as sickles and sythes, and for cutlery. Blades were sharpened on a vertically revolving grindstone, the iron-work processes having been carried out elsewhere. This had become a Birmingham speciality in the 16th century and large numbers of the mills in the countryside around the town were converted for blade production. Over Mill was a blade mill by 1624 when William Hunt, a Deritend bladesmith, was in occupation, and Pebble Mill was probably converted by 1648. The Civil War gave a great boost to the pro-duction of swords and knives in these mills.

13 Edgbaston Mill: in the late 19th century this was still a corn mill. The house was demolished only recently.

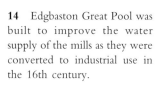

14 Edgbaston Great Pool was built to improve the water supply of the mills as they were converted to industrial use in the 16th century.

In the 19th century they changed to other production processes. Speedwell was being used for producing inlaid and steel buttons in 1785, for gun barrels in 1810, as a wire mill in 1823, and for brass and copper tube making in 1845. The mill was demolished with the construction of Princess Road in the 1860s. Pebble Mill was still used for cutlery in the 1830s, but had reverted to a corn mill in 1842 when Joseph Flecknoe, a baker and flour dealer, took over.

Milling ceased in 1890. Over Mill was a rolling mill in 1836 for the gold and silversmith Samuel Horton, John Spurrier doing the skilled work in the mill until the 1850s. The mill was still standing in the 1930s, but has now been demolished. Finally, Edgbaston Mill remained as the corn mill for the parish until the 1880s when it was used as the farmhouse for a dairy farm. The attractive mill house was demolished only a few years ago.

Four

Mansion, Park and the Calthorpes

The Gough and Calthorpe Families

The two daughters of Lady Gage, daughter of Robert Middlemore, sold the estates at Edgbaston to Sir Richard Gough (1659-1727) in 1717 for £20,400. Sir Richard's nephew, Harry, bought the other Middlemore estates in Warwickshire and Worcestershire for £13,000. Sir Richard was a London merchant trading in the Levant. He then made four lucrative voyages to the East Indies and became a director of the East India Company, a Whig MP (for Bramber in Sussex), and a landowner. He was knighted in 1715 and he purchased Edgbaston for his 'retirement' into the landed gentry. This change in ownership of the Edgbaston estate is important because it provides us with two maps. For the first time we can be certain how the landscape of most of the parish was laid out, where the buildings were, and who farmed what areas.

The first map was drawn in 1701 by William Deeley to enable the estate to be fairly divided between the Gage daughters. It therefore shows only the Gage lands. They did not own land to the north of the Hagley Road and there were three other estates intruding into their total control of the parish south of the Hagley Road; there was one area beside the Bourn Brook, where the university and King Edward's School are now located, another in the vicinity of Lee Bank, and a third stretching from the Hagley Road down to the *White Swan Inn*. This last block was the farms of Mr Jennens and the Rev. Dr Smallbrook. Most of the farms were of 50-60 acres or less but Philip Loxley,

who seems to have been the tenant of Edgbaston Hall at this time, though he lived in the farmhouse at the bottom of Wheeley's Lane, had a holding almost three times this size. The other important holding was Poole's Farm, the holding stretching from Metchley Park eastwards to beyond Edgbaston Pool and up the hill to the Hall. Its farmhouse was where 'The Elms' stands, at the junction of Somerset and Edgbaston Park Roads. Most farms were compact blocks of land, the only exception being the riverside meadows where some farmers had a valuable meadow that was some distance from their main farm. A number of widows rented single fields where they were able to keep a few cows. This enabled them to supply Birmingham residents with milk and so make their living and avoid the poor house.

The second map was drawn in 1717, for Sir Richard Gough when he purchased the estate, by Humphrey Sparry. It shows the whole of Edgbaston parish and therefore fills in the 'missing' portions of the 1701 plan. It is sufficiently detailed for us to count the 64 houses scattered across the parish and land can be allocated to the 33 farm holdings. We can see that some farms spanned the Hagley Road and its different land ownership and were not as small as they appear to have been in 1701. We can see, too, how some of the holdings in the east of the parish were already smaller as more Birmingham residents sought out smallholdings, and how quite large fields in 1701 were being sub-divided into smaller fields suitable for livestock. Finally, we can see a typical process of settlement expansion for this period in the number of cottages that have been built on the former heathland where the north end of Metchley Park, Harborne Heath and the Chad valley meet at Harborne Hill. There were others where what is now Hermitage Road meets Hagley Road, which was another area of waste, and still more taking in small plots from the roadside of Hagley Road itself.

Sir Richard died in 1727, and was succeded by his eldest son, Henry (1708-74), who was created a baronet the following year. Sir Henry's wife died childless in 1740 and two

years later he married Barbara Calthorpe, heiress to some 2,000 acres of Norfolk, a house at Ampton, Suffolk, and another at Elvetham, Hampshire, since both her brother and the only other two male relatives were unmarried. Sir Henry died in 1774, leaving Edgbaston to their eldest son, also Henry (Lady Barbara had borne him six children). Barbara died in 1782, and her brother in 1788, leaving the Calthorpe estates to Sir Henry Gough II who, as was usual in these circumstances, adopted the extinct name to become Henry Gough-Calthorpe. The following year he requested a peerage from the Prime Minister, but it was to be 1796 before

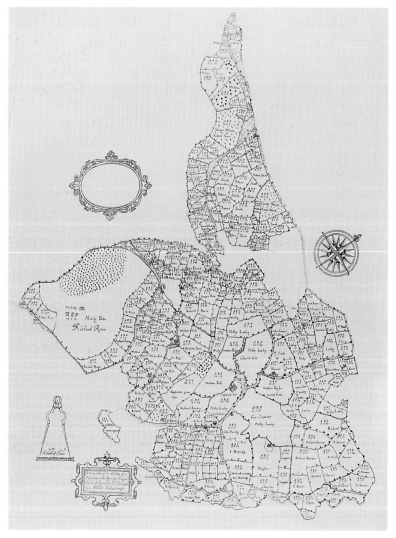

15 Deeley's plan, 1701: this plan and survey enabled the Middlemore lands to be fairly divided between the female heirs.

16 Cottages were being built on Harborne Heath from the 17th century. This row in Nursery Road probably dates from the early 19th century.

17 Sir Richard Gough: Sir Richard moved from merchant to landed squire; a portrait was a social necessity in his new role.

he was enobled as Baron Calthorpe of Calthorpe, Norfolk. The 1st Lord Calthorpe lived only two more years but, unusually, his will gave his successors the right to sell off the agricultural estates in Norfolk provided they invested the proceeds in consolidating their other estates in Edgbaston or Elvetham. Charles, 2nd Baron Calthorpe (1786-1806) died young, leaving the estates to his younger brother George (1787-1851), and it was he who set in train the events which were to transform the fortunes of the family, and of the parish of Edgbaston.

Edgbaston Park

We know little about the house and gardens of Edgbaston Hall before the early 18th century. Presumably, whatever was there was badly damaged in the Civil War fighting and the destruction of 1688. However, Deeley's map of 1701 shows a typical three-bay gabled Elizabe-

than house with a barn yard adjoining the church, suggesting that at least the outer walls of the hall were still standing and that it had been re-roofed. By 1717, Sparry's plan shows the classical house that still stands there and which was built by Sir Richard Gough as soon as he purchased the estate (though seemingly using some parts of the old hall). The Little Park consisted only of a field south from the house beside Priory Road, with the fish stew ponds beside the road and a small belt of woodland in the south-west corner. The Great Pool is present in 1701 and, since the northern end is both silted and wooded, had clearly existed for at least a century or more. Finally, even in 1701, a shelter-belt or avenue called 'the Grove' sheltered the house from cold north-easterly winds.

These features are confirmed by Henry Beighton's fine engraving of 1730, which shows the grove of mature trees to the north and the stew ponds beside Priory Road in more detail.

When Sir Richard Gough acquired the estate he not only built himself a new house but also enclosed and planted new formal gardens in the Little Park, which he surrounded with a timber palisade fence and stocked with deer in 1719. Beighton's engraving of the house and park shows the house surrounded by level lawns with an open timber fence around it on top of a substantial bank with a central set of steps. One avenue of large conifers leads south, on either side of the steps, and another north-east to the farm buildings; a third avenue branches from this to the parish church. In the foreground is a close-planted geometrical garden of young trees and shrubs. On the north side of the house a semi-circular gravelled coach entrance leads to another straight tree-lined path to the kitchen garden, where fan-trained fruit trees against the wall are in evidence. More formal avenues go down the slope to the Great Pool. A number of magnificent sweet chestnut trees are still to be found in the woods here next to Edgbaston Park Road. They were a fashionable tree in 17th-century gardens and may date from that period.

In 1776, two years after inheriting the estate, Sir Henry Gough II commissioned England's foremost landscape gardener,

'Capability' Brown, to provide designs for his park, but it is unclear whether he visited Edgbaston, or what the nature of the designs he provided were. However, the features that characterise Brown's designs were certainly present at Edgbaston Park by the time William Withering took a lease on the property in 1789. By Brown's standards, the 141 acres of the park was small, but it had a varied topography and a large lake. The likelihood must be that Brown suggested the refurbishment and, perhaps, raising of the dam to improve it somewhat. The deep shelter-belt of beech trees beyond the pool is characteristic of Brown's designs and was not present in 1730. They are now an important nature reserve. A ha-ha, or sunken ditch (another characteristic Brown design feature), replaced the embankment and fence around the house, and the avenues were removed, though many individual trees were probably kept. Further shelter-belt planting took place along the Priory Road boundary, where again Brown's characteristic beech trees are prominent. Finally the kitchen garden was fully walled to hide it from the house and laid out with six compartments divided by paths.

William Withering was able to lease the hall and park in 1786 because Sir Henry had

18 Edgbaston Hall and park in 1730: the new brick mansion and its surrounding gardens, avenues and woodlands were illustrated in the second edition of Dugdale.

19 *Above left*. This little 18th-century Gothick estate cottage stands in Edgbaston Park Road and now belongs to the University.

20 *Above right*. Edgbaston Hall in around 1810: this painting shows the hall in a more 'Romantic' light, embowered by trees.

21 *Right*. Portrait of Dr William Withering.

decided to live at Elvetham Hall in Hampshire. Withering's 14-year lease cost him £237 10s. per year, with an additional £10 payable if he converted the park to tillage. Amongst other things he had to restock the Great Pool with carp or tench as fish were removed, showing us that the pool was used for fishing up to this time. He was unable to sub-let the property and there was a break clause after seven years if Sir Henry wished to re-occupy the hall. However, the Gough-Calthorpes were never to return to live in Edgbaston as, through their own development policies, it became increasingly suburbanised. Withering clearly liked his park, writing in 1791, 'The verdure of the park is more vivid this spring than I have ever seen it before, the large cherry trees are white with blossoms and the chestnuts are protruding their gaudy spikes.' Withering was succeeded by another doctor, Edward Johnstone (1805-51). Then, in the 1850s, the third tenant of the hall, John Whateley, made a new entrance on the other side of the church with a pretty classical brick lodge and attractive ornamental brick walls which still survive.

22 William Withering memorial in Edgbaston old
church.

23 *An Account of the Foxglove*: William Withering's
book was a path-breaking medical and botanical volume.

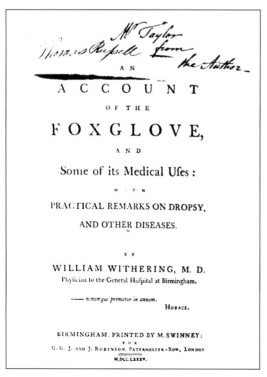

William Withering and the 1791 Riots

Dr William Withering, MD, FRS, FLS was
perhaps Edgbaston Hall's most famous tenant.
He was the only son of an apothecary in
Wellington, Shropshire; he trained as a physician
in Edinburgh and took his first post in Stafford
Infirmary in 1766. He left to come to
Birmingham thanks to the intervention of
Erasmus Darwin, joining the town's most
distinguished medical practice. Whilst at Stafford
he wrote a book in two volumes on *The
Botanical Arrangement of all the Vegetables Naturally Growing in Great Britain*. It was published
soon after he arrived in Birmingham and his
fame as a naturalist spread rapidly. Two further
editions were published in 1787 and 1796 and
a centenary 14th edition was successfully
published in 1877. He was elected a Fellow of
the Linnean Society and followed with another
book, *An Account of the Foxglove*, which is
celebrated as both the first treatise on the
scientific treatment of disease written in English
and the first book to specify the diuretic
properties of digitalis. Fellowship of the Royal
Society followed, and he became both rich and
famous since he was an extremely good
physician in an age when they were in
notoriously short supply. He died in 1799, aged
only 58, as he was preparing to move to a
smaller house and a warmer location in
Sparkbrook. He was buried at Edgbaston church
where there is a memorial on the wall to his
memory.

The riots of July 1791 are an important
part of Birmingham's political and social history;
Edgbaston Hall is where they ended. Their
cause was the tension between Anglican church-
men and Dissenters who were trying to repeal
the Corporation and Test Laws at this time so
that they could play a fuller part in society.
The spark was a dinner held to celebrate the
French Revolution which enabled a mob to
be whipped into a fury by pamphlets and
speeches. Destruction began with the burning
of Birmingham's two Dissenting chapels. The
mob then went through Digbeth to attack the

24 Hay-making in Meadow Road: though a much later view, Withering's furniture could have been hidden quickly under such a cartload of hay.

25 The Dining Room, Edgbaston Hall, in 1926.

home of Joseph Priestley in Sparkbrook, which was totally destroyed along with most of his papers and scientific equipment. Next day several houses in Birmingham were burnt and then the mob went out into the surrounding countryside attacking houses in Bordesley, Sparkbrook, Wake Green and Moseley Hall. Edgbaston Hall was next on the rioters' list.

The events of Saturday and Sunday 16–17 July are described in detail in a letter that Withering sent to Lord Calthorpe three days afterwards. On Saturday morning he had sent his gardener to mix with the 300 or more rioters

in Moseley and discovered that the intention was to set fire to the hall on Sunday evening. The servants in the hall began moving the furniture and fittings out of the house. Three cart- and two wagon-loads had been removed to the comparative safety of the church when about 250 men were spotted on their way from Moseley to plunder the house. The last wagon-load of valuables had to be driven into the hayfield and covered with hay to disguise it. Bribes and a lot of alcohol persuaded the mob to go away, and by evening more of Withering's possessions had been cleared from the house

26 Perrot's Folly was built in 1758, an early example of a Gothick folly.

into the church where they were guarded by some of his men. The mob returned and took over the house, but again bribes, drink and some strong-arm tactics removed them by morning. On the Sunday morning, after Moseley Hall had been destroyed, Withering's butler seems to have successfully led the drunken mob away from Edgbaston and they spent much of the afternoon sleeping off the effects of drink. Finally, however, some 300 men arrived at Edgbaston at 8 p.m. intent on arson. Withering was popular in Birmingham and he seems to have had little trouble in recruiting his own force of friends and pugilists to defend his

property. More bribes, drink, and the promise of more in the *Bell Inn* persuaded most to leave, and the remaining 30 were no match for the hall's defenders, though the fighting continued for some hours. The ringleaders were locked in one of the outhouses to await the military, who arrived in Birmingham next morning, having ridden from Nottingham overnight. For a week afterwards the house and out-buildings were watched nightly, but it was then considered safe to return the contents from the church. Only 12 men faced trial at Warwick Assizes for these events and only four were found guilty.

Rotton Park

To the north of Hagley Road, Rotton Park was also developed as a rural estate in the 18th century. It had been sold to Humphrey Perrot of Belbroughton in 1628. Two farms were sold in 1689-70, including 59 acres beside the Hagley Road. In 1758 John Perrot built the strange seven-storied brick tower, ever since known as Perrot's Folly, on the highest part of the estate, which gave name to the later Monument Road. It may have been an architectural 'eye-catcher' from the Perrot mansion; another suggestion is that it was for watching hare coursing, a sport beloved by Perrot. John died in 1774 and the estate was inherited by his daughter, who had married Walter Noel. The house was let and the advertisement provides a good description of the gardens. There was 'a dovehouse, coach-house, good stabling, gardens well-planted with the best fruits, a neat shrubbery, and about ten acres of land in high condition'. The folly was used by the Birmingham and Midland Institute from 1887 for meteorological observations, which continued for more than a century.

Five

Building the Suburb: Houses and Villas

The original estate purchased by Sir Richard Gough had consisted of 1,700 acres of Edgbaston's 2,500 acres. By 1787 further purchases had increased this to nearly 2,000 acres. By 1819 only the 88 acres of the Curzon estate intruded into the Calthorpe acres to the south of the Hagley Road and this was purchased for £18,500 in that year. The first building leases were granted in 1786 in the triangle of land between Hagley and Harborne Roads at Five Ways. They were for 99 years, specified a minimum value for the houses to be built (£400 in the first instance), insisted that the plans be vetted by the estate's agent, and provided for a fixed ground rent. These conditions ensured that only people of an appropriate social class would be able to build in Edgbaston which was, in almost all respects, the ideal location for middle-class suburban residential development. It was to the south-west of the city, so prevailing winds would blow away smoke and polluted air; it stood high and had a gravelly soil, so the land was well-drained and provided views out to the surrounding countryside, and the park and pastoral farming ensured that there were already mature trees to enhance those prospects still further; finally, the single landowner ensured that no-one was able to disrupt the social homogeneity by building working-class housing or industrial buildings.

Building plans really began to develop after the depression years of the Napoleonic wars after George, the 3rd Lord, had acceded to the title.

Practicalities were largely in the hands of John Harris, Lord Calthorpe's agent in Edgbaston. Progress in attracting the right sort of people seemed painfully slow at the time but, by 1842, 342 building leases had been completed, mostly for land in the eastern part of the parish, and the estate rental had more than doubled. So as to

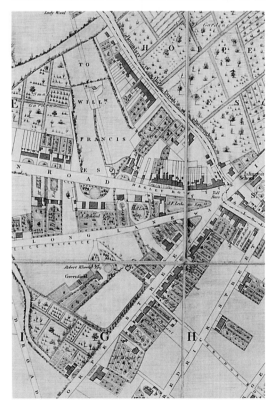

27 Piggott-Smith's map (1824-5) shows the early development at Five Ways and the occupants of all the houses.

28 Regency houses in Hagley Road.

encourage building, farmers had first to be moved to holdings in the west of the parish as lands became available and, secondly, new streets and drains had to be laid down as a framework for building. The first two areas saw Calthorpe, George, Frederick and Church Roads laid out in the Five Ways district, and Wellington and Sir Harry's Road constructed to the south-east, all before 1820. These were followed by Westbourne, Vicarage and Chad Roads in the 1820s. Constructing the roads did not, of course, see the instant building of houses along their length and it was to be many years before all these roads were fully built up; only in the Five Ways corner of the estate were there continuous lines of properties along the streets. In an industrial town such as Birmingham it was inevitable that building new houses closely followed the economic cycle; if business was flourishing businessmen built themselves fashionable new houses, but in times of depression there was little construction.

Rapid Expansion

The second phase of development, between 1842 and 1880, were years of almost continuous expansion and at three times the rate of the first half of the century. By 1880, 1,077 leases had been granted, estate income had risen to £30,000 per year, and the population of Edgbaston rose from 6,600 in 1841 to 22,700

in 1881. New areas of development were underway along Ampton and Carpenter Roads in the core of the estate, to the south of Hagley Road along Augustus, Norfolk and Westfield Roads, and west of the Chad Brook, along Somerset, Farquhar and Richmond Hill Roads. Edgbaston boomed as the economy of Birmingham boomed. In 1881 the first issue of *Edgbastonia* could declare without fear of contradiction that 'Edgbaston is unquestionably the fashionable suburb of Birmingham. The fact that the land is the property of one man, who will permit none but first-class houses to be erected, renders it the favourite site for the residences of independent persons and the wealthier classes of professional men, merchants and traders.' But after 1880 building slumped and only 206 more leases were granted on the Calthorpe estate before 1914; one notable development was the demolition of 'Greenfield' on its seven-acre plot in the 1880s and the building of Greenfield Crescent on the site. There was still 1,000 acres of farmland to develop and Birmingham was continuing to expand rapidly around and beyond Edgbaston, but the suburb stagnated as other places became fashionable and had more modern houses, and as motor cars enabled wealthy people to live in rural Knowle or Solihull and still be able to travel in to work each day. As they leap-frogged beyond Edgbaston the bus, tram and vehicle

29 Houses in George Road, *c*.1820.

traffic using the Bristol and Hagley Roads began to increase rapidly and they became busy commuter thoroughfares by the end of the 19th century, further devaluing Edgbaston as the resort of the wealthy.

The houses built between 1800 and 1914 reflected closely the architectural styles that succeeded one another through the century. There were dignified classical terraces of 1810 along Hagley Road. Then came more spectacular villas and semi-detached houses, stuccoed and in classical styles from the 1820s along Calthorpe and Highfield Roads. Many of these houses had the cast-iron balconies and porches characteristic of the Regency period; they are especially notable in Vicarage Road. Smaller Georgian or Regency-style terraces were also built to the west of Lee Bank, including Lee Crescent. Most of these dwellings were on quite small plots of only half an acre or so, but some larger ornamental villas were also built in this style, such as 'Park Grove' on the Bristol Road. By the end of the first phase of development in the 1840s, most houses were larger and built in a more severe neo-classical style with columned porticos and spacious rooms, and with the houses set well back from the street, such as some of those in Wellington Road. The 'battle of the styles' in the 1860s and '70s is well represented in Edgbaston, large Italianate mansions vying for attention with tall

neo-Gothic houses often in polychrome brick. Next comes the Elizabethan brickwork, tile-hanging and timber-framing of the early Arts and Crafts period from the 1880s, and the innovative houses of Birmingham's finest exponents of this style in the first decade of the new century. These include Tudor Buckland's houses in Yateley Road, including no. 21, which he designed for himself in 1899. Equally notable are the delightful lodge buildings which mark the entrance drives of the largest houses, which range from plain neo-classical to tiny Gothic castles. Often these have survived where the mansion has long since been demolished.

Maintaining Standards

The perception, both in the 19th century and today, that Edgbaston was entirely occupied by the middle classes and their bespoke houses is not wholly correct. Quite early in the development process the Calthorpes and their agents evolved a policy of social zoning whereby the most exclusive houses of the industrial aristocracy, set in the largest gardens, were located in the centre of the estate nearest to the hall and church; more middling middle-class houses surrounded them in a crescent on the town-ward side; whilst areas for the 'labour aristocracy' protected the estate close to the densely developed courtyard slums of Ladywood, Lee Bank and Balsall Heath. These latter were developed by speculative builders in terraces, but with very generous gardens. The first of these areas was to the north of Hagley Road where Beaufort, Duchess and Francis Roads were built from the late 1840s through to the mid-1850s. In the 1860s development began in the south-east corner of the estate where the damp meadows of the Rea would not have been appreciated by the better off. Here a large estate between the Pershore Road, Calthorpe Park and the river began to be built, but houses were still being in-filled here in the first decade of the 20th century.

It was, of course, in these areas that the estate had to fight hardest to maintain the ban on commercial establishments and workshops. Many occupants tried to open businesses: a moneylender, a dressmaker and even a fish and chip shop (in Varna Road) had to be dealt with in the first decade of the 20th century; a farmer had unthinkingly offered his land for the tent of 'Sanger's Circus' in 1874 and this required a court injunction to stop it; even the corporation was remiss in allowing a public urinal to be erected on the corner of Speed-well Road for the comfort of those visiting Calthorpe Park. In the more salubrious parts of the suburb residents were self-policing and even the hint of something untoward would have resulted in a letter to the agent requesting him to take action. Such problems got more severe

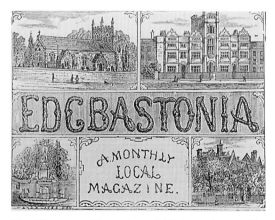

30 The cover illustration of Edgbaston's monthly magazine.

as the earliest leases near to Five Ways began to revert to the Calthorpes at a time when the estate, in common with many others in England, was having to harvest its financial resources very carefully. It therefore began to sell some land to institutions on the outer fringes of the estate, the Blue Coat School for example, whilst at Five Ways the commercial possibilities were already proving tempting. One property company wished to erect apartment blocks there, and another to build a cinema. The estate was all set to grant this proposal permission for a lease of £150 but, when it became known, there was an outcry from Edgbaston's residents, a protest meeting, petitions, and scores of letters to the estate office, so the proposal was quietly shelved. Shops were already serving the suburb, since a splendid terrace had been built at the *Ivy Bush* in the 1880s, but they were on the other side of the Hagley Road.

In the inter-war period of the 20th century the development potential of the estate quietly mouldered. There was some redevelopment of properties, some commercial buildings were finally allowed, and a number of institutions given room on the remaining farmland of the south-west of the estate. Commercial property was built at Five Ways, including the delightful Edwardian Lloyd's Bank designed by P.B. Chatwin in 1908-9, and other houses nearby were occupied by professional firms such as solicitors and doctors. Luxury apartment blocks were built on Hagley and Bristol Roads at Kenilworth Court and Viceroy Close respectively, whilst some of the larger mansions at the heart of the estate were demolished and replaced with fashionable Art Deco houses in the 1930s.

Finally, any story of development needs to take notice of the estate to the north of the Hagley Road. This was in the hands of the Noel family in the early 19th century. In 1852 it was purchased by Joseph Gillott, the Birmingham pen manufacturer, for what was then regarded as the sensational price of £100,000. He lived in Westbourne Road,

31 Regency terrace in Carpenter Road with characteristic cast-iron porches.

32 C.H. Blood's map, 1857: this map clearly shows the rural fringe of Edgbaston in the mid–19th century.

33 Neo-classical house in Wellington Road.

34 Italianate Neo-classical, Church Road.

35 Arts and Crafts, No. 21 Yateley Road: built by Tudor Buckland, for himself, 1899. He continued to live in this house until his death in 1951. Today it has been carefully restored and is a Grade I Listed Building.

36 *Above left*. Neo-Gothic (by Chamberlain & Martin), Carpenter Road.

37 *Above right*. Arts & Crafts (by W.H. Bidlake), Farquhar Road.

38 & 39 Lodge cottages in Westbourne Road. *Right*. built in 1870 as the lodge to 'Oak Mount'. *Below*. The lodge to 'Ashleigh', *c*.1860.

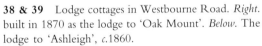

40 Kenilworth Court: luxury apartments on the Hagley Road built in the 1930s.

41 Part of the Gillott estate: St Augustine's Church is in the centre; Hagley Road to the bottom right; the intersection of Portland and Rotton Park Roads to the top left. Redevelopment for apartments and offices was already underway by the early 1970s.

Edgbaston and though he clearly bought the land for speculative building, he developed his estate in the same way as the Calthorpes were developing their outer fringe, that is to say for the lower middle class and the labour aristocracy. By 1890 the area as far west as the Harborne railway line had been developed to a depth of several hundred yards back from the Hagley Road, and St Augustine's Church had been constructed to serve the estate. There was another group of houses at the western end of the estate where Bearwood was beginning to develop around the crossroads at the *King's Head* inn. Building began along Poplar Road and Barnsley Road was developed in the first decade of the 20th century by the builders of that name, who had been active in Edgbaston throughout the previous century.

Six

Gardens and Parks

It is estimated that Edgbaston contains over a million trees. A high proportion of these were planted by the first occupants of the mansions and villas as they developed their gardens, and there are both rarities and very large specimens of forest trees now grown to maturity. Some of these trees are planted on the embanked soil inside boundary walls so that they overhang the roads. It is these trees, not street planting, that gives Edgbaston its tree-dominated streetscapes. The other dominating street features are boundary walls, gate pillars and lodges. The majority of the walls are brick-built but another distinctive building material is furnace slag brought in from the Black Country by boat along the canal. The estate made a conscious effort to preserve walls and trees when large parts were redeveloped in the 1960s and '70s.

Domestic Gardens

Only recently have we begun to realise that Edgbaston preserves quite rare features of 19th-century domestic gardens. Boundary walls, perimeter gravel paths (sometimes sinuous, sometimes straight), ornamental features such as fountains, rock work, lawns (including tennis lawns), and trees, together with stables, conservatories and greenhouses, are all preserved from the period. Some of the best preservation is in those properties that were given over to institutional use in the 20th century. These include 'The Firs', an 1830s house which became the Midland Nerve Hospital and, recently, a university student residence complex, but which preserves many of the features and trees of its Regency garden, and 'Oakhurst', built c.1835, and since 1952 the Birmingham School of Speech Training and Dramatic Art,

42   Ampton and Arthur Roads: an example of 'furnace slag' walls with embanked planting and mature forest trees.

33

43 'Wyddrington', Church Road: this house had some of the most renowned gardens in late 19th-century Edgbaston.

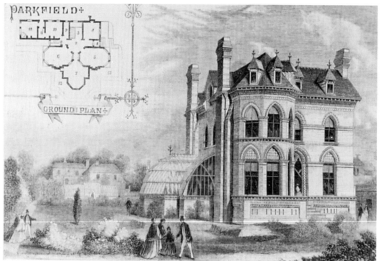

44 'Parkfield', Pershore Road: this sale brochure shows all the elements of a high Victorian garden: terrace, conservatory, greenhouse, gravel paths, shrubberies and specimen trees.

which preserves even more of a Regency garden layout, including a crinkle-crankle wall beside the canal.

Equally interesting is the contemporary description of his garden by James Luckock in 1828. He lived at 'Lime Grove' at the end of George Road, a house which looked out over the canal. In his one-third of an acre he developed a garden in conscious imitation of Shenstone's 'The Leasowes'. It had seats and statues alongside the paths 'inscribed with suitable verses', and a grotto. The statues included a life-sized goddess Ceres. In his borders he grew 'old peonies, Brompton stocks,

lilies, tulips and snowdrops' and there was a formal rose garden. In a small orchard he had damsons, pears, currants, plums, apples and gooseberries, and a hedge of filbert nuts. The soil was manured with sifted ash, soot, green refuse 'and slops from the wash-tub'. Luckock tells us he ran it for £10-12 a year and that he employed a part-time gardener. The plot was redeveloped in 1969.

A number of other 'period' gardens are to be found. These include the Arts and Crafts garden at 21 Yateley Road, restored after Tudor Buckland's death in 1951 by its new owners. It had spectacular rhododendron banks and crisscrossing flights of steps up the slope, a formal rose garden, and an extensive fruit and vegetable garden which was a significant part of the self-sufficiency ideals of the members of the movement. 'Avonmore', in Church Road, was rebuilt in 1934-5 in Art Deco style and the garden remodelled at the same time with a broad terrace, rose garden with a contemporary fountain, and a sunken garden, whilst 'Ravensburg', in Westbourne Road, was demolished and rebuilt in 1932 and, again, has a contemporary garden with a brick pergola, crazy paving, and a large stone terrace with pools and seats. Finally, there are modern 'plantsman's' gardens in Edgbaston, some of which open to the public under the National Gardens Scheme.

Nursery Gardens

One of the very few commercial businesses the Calthorpes were prepared to allow in Edgbaston was nursery gardens. R.H. Vertigans ran the Chad Valley Nursery in Harborne Road, opposite the *White Swan*, in the 1850s and advertised his landscaping services as well as his plants, trees and shrubs. This was still a nursery

until the 1960s when it was occupied by Simpson's seed merchants. In 1872 Thomas Cowdry was advertising himself as 'landscape gardener, nurseryman and contractor' for the 'laying out of parks, arboretums, pleasure grounds, fish pools, rockwork and gardens of every description'. The 'Holly Nursery', in Hermitage Road, was especially long-lived since it was at the western end of the estate.

Guinea Gardens

Agricultural land in the vicinity of growing towns is often subject to new, more profitable, uses as the edge of the town gets ever closer until, eventually, it gets developed for building. In the mid-18th century, one of these uses in the vicinity of Birmingham and other developing industrial cities involved dividing fields into small plots and letting them, on yearly tenancies, as allotments on which town dwellers could grow vegetables, fruit and flowers. The usual rent for these allotments was between 17s. 6d. and 30 shillings, but one guinea was especially common and they were often known as 'guinea gardens' in consequence. Birmingham

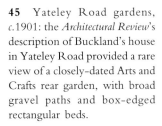

45 Yateley Road gardens, *c*.1901: the *Architectural Review*'s description of Buckland's house in Yateley Road provided a rare view of a closely-dated Arts and Crafts rear garden, with broad gravel paths and box-edged rectangular beds.

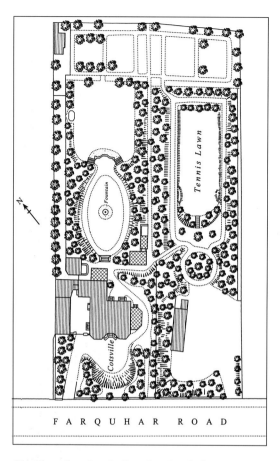

46   Plan of gardens in Farquhar Road: the 1:500 scale Ordnance Survey plan shows the detailed layout of Edgbaston gardens in the 1880s.

was ringed by such guinea gardens on all sides into the early 19th century and they were especially prevalent on the western side, where the fields at the eastern extremities of Edgbaston were being let in this way. The pages of Birmingham's newspaper, *Aris's Gazette*, are full of advertisements for these gardens from the 1760s onwards. In 1765, for example, the creation of such a garden near Holloway Head is reported, there being 'two rows of gardens with a walk nine feet wide between them'; they were to be let at 2s. 10d. per rod. Later the gardens are sold with all their plants, so, in 1797, one was to be sold at auction where 'the soil is remarkably rich and full of manure; the

vegetables and hot-bed plants in very great forwardness; the fruits are all of the best and in their prime'. In 1812 one was offered 'well planted with gooseberry and currant trees, fine raspberries, flowers, shrubs, etc., and stocked with asparagus and vegetables of various kinds, containing a summer house'. Fine flowers were grown on other plots, including tulips, carnations, and auriculas in pots (all of which plants were popular subjects in flower shows in Regency England).

The gardens were usually hedged or fenced and often contained brick summer houses or wooden sheds to contain gardening tools. Clearly, as with modern allotment gardens, for some people these plots were little rural oases where they could escape from the grime and smoke of the town on a regular basis; for others they were places where fresh fruit and vegetables could be grown to supplement the diet, or as supplementary income since such produce could easily be sold in the Bull Ring market. The only clear illustration of these gardens comes from J. Piggott-Smith's fine plan of Birmingham, engraved in 1824-5. This shows that landowners had leased large areas east of Lee Bank for guinea gardens, whilst Lord Calthorpe was doing the same to the west in Edgbaston: they lined each side of the Worcester Canal south of George Street, there was a little block north of the Hagley Road at Five Ways, and there was a very large block of gardens between Hagley Road and Harborne Road, west of Highfield Road. Loudon noted them when he came to Birmingham to design the Botanical Gardens, and registered his surprise in his *Gardener's Magazine* at the variety of hardy shrubs that were being grown. He also noted that when they were sold they fetched an average of 20 guineas, but could fetch up to 60 guineas.

The inner-city ring of guinea gardens has long since disappeared but in Westbourne Road there still remain today the last few plots of this kind in Birmingham. The Westbourne Road gardens were created in 1844 on land given up by the Botanical Gardens. Since there were

47 The Beadle's House, Ampton Road: this much-extended house possibly dates from the late 17th century. In the 19th century it was a nursery.

48 Part of J. Piggott-Smith's plan of Birmingham, 1824-5: the band of guinea gardens in Edgbaston, Ladywood and Lee Bank is well shown.

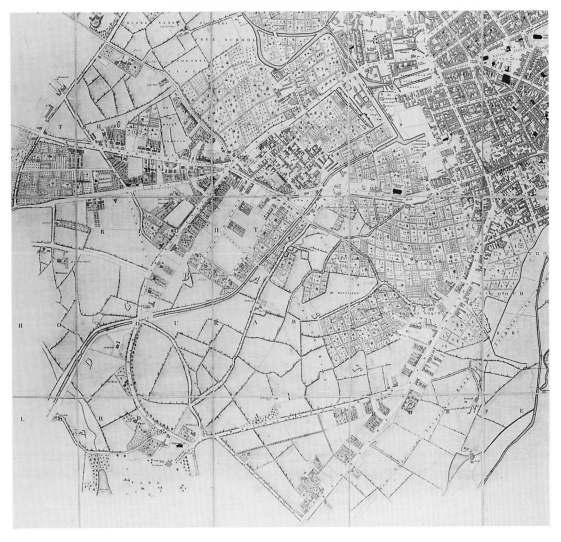

49 Allotment gardens, Yateley Road: allotments are the modern successors to guinea gardens but are rarely as tidy or productive.

already established fruit trees and vegetable grounds, it was an obvious use for this otherwise inaccessible plot and Lord Calthorpe laid out 250 garden plots, mostly of one-eighth of an acre. A few gardens were lost when the railway line was doubled in the 1880s, 30 more were taken by the playing fields of the High School for Girls in 1960, 17 were taken by the archery and tennis club, and 20 were reclaimed by the Botanical Gardens. Six of these were remodelled by the BBC as part of their 'Gardening Club' series, which continued until 1968, after which the site was cleared. Eighty-seven plots remain in Westbourne Gardens today; sadly, the lease came under the management of the city council in 1964 and, in 1971-2, they were badly damaged when almost all the fruit trees and many of the hedges were wantonly removed and all but one of the brick summer houses demolished. Only one plot now retains the traditional elaborate path design in bricks or gravel. They are now listed Grade II by English Heritage and there are plans to restore one of them to its original appearance, but their future is still in doubt as the lease from the Calthorpe estate is due for renegotiation in 2002.

Public Parks

Calthorpe Park, on Pershore Road, was one of Birmingham's first two public parks, laid out in 1856-7. As in many other industrial cities, middle-class citizens became concerned at the lack of green spaces and opportunities for recreation for working-class people increasingly confined to overcrowded, insanitary, back-to-back courtyard houses. One response to this concern was a call for municipalities to provide freely available 'green lungs' of grass and trees for all who wished to avail themselves of the opportunity of walking and recreation. Since the town council did not wish to spend large sums of ratepayers' money on purchasing land for parks, they were reliant on the public-spiritedness of landowners on the city fringes. Lord Norton, who gifted Adderley Park to the town, and Lord Calthorpe were the first to respond. Lord Calthorpe's proposal was in the form of a year-long experiment whereby he proposed to lease the council the 20-30 acres of land required for a park for £3 per annum. However, his lack of understanding of the lives of working people is revealed in a stipulation that the park should not be open on Sundays, which was the main day on which poorer people could have enjoyed its facilities; but he was rather ahead of his times in requesting that dogs be banned and that smoking should not be allowed within its bounds! After some negotiation these restrictions were removed, the rent increased to £5 per annum, and the land laid out by the council for the use of the public.

The park was officially opened by HRH The Duke of Cambridge on 1 June 1857. Three *Cedrus deodara* trees were planted in the centre of the park by the duke, the mayor, and Lord Calthorpe respectively. Subsequently, in 1871, Lord Calthorpe gifted the land to the council, though not before an altercation over the fact that they had allowed bicycling in the park in violation of the covenants. The park stretched between Speedwell Road and Edward Road, and from the Pershore Road to the River Rea. Trees were planted around its perimeter and a drive laid out across it aligned on Varna Road. There was an octagonal refreshments pavilion in the middle of the main drive and the inevitable bandstand at the junction of the two main paths. There was a lodge for the park keeper on the corner of Speedwell Road and Pershore Road, with fine cast-iron entrance gates and iron palisading along the Pershore Road frontage. There were oak pale fences on the other road frontages. After 1871 the council also added shrubberies and flower beds near the entrance gates and beside the perimeter path, but most of the park was open grassland. This made it extremely popular with cricket and football clubs on the south-west side of the city. By 1900 diagonal crosswalks had been added and the bandstand was surrounded by a large circular gravelled area where seats could be laid out for those listening to band performances. Unfortunately, the park had been divided into two unequal portions, linked by bridges, by the straightening and culverting of the River Rea to prevent flooding.

Birmingham's premier park at Cannon Hill is usually reckoned in Edgbaston but in fact the only part within the historic parish is the Nature

50 Plan of Calthorpe Park, 1892: the city prepared a survey of all their public parks in 1892, complete with detailed plans.

51 Calthorpe Park, 1916: the western end of the park was well planted, though the flower beds were interspersed with tennis courts.

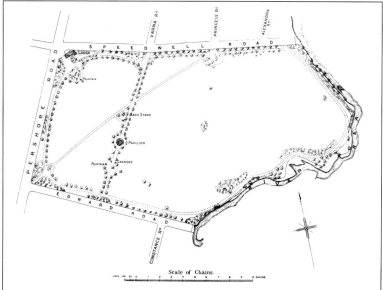

52   The Botanical Gardens, 1874: the original glasshouses, main lawn and bandstand can be seen in this engraving.

Centre on Pershore Road, the main part of the park is in Moseley.

Birmingham Botanical Gardens

Edgbaston is uniquely endowed with two botanical gardens of national significance, one still independently owned and the other the property of the University of Birmingham. Botanical gardens were being newly established in quite large numbers in the early 19th century. This was a consequence of a growing middle-class interest in scientific botany and the cultivation of the enormous range of exotic plants that were being brought back to Britain from the furthest reaches of empire. This in turn stimulated a growing interest in gardening, especially as the role of women in middle-class households was increasingly seen as confined to the domestic (including the garden) and the family.

The Birmingham Botanical Gardens were laid out for the Birmingham Botanical and Horticultural Society, which had been formed in 1829. Its committee investigated a number of possible sites, commissioning an experienced local gardener, Mr Lunn, to undertake the task.

His choice was 12½ acres of ground on the south side of Westbourne Road which, he reported, 'contains a mixture of soil, suitable for Botanical and Horticultural purposes … a small brook … a bold southern aspect … and has a pleasing view of Edgbaston Hall, and an extensive view of the surrounding country'.

Next the committee appointed a curator and gardener, David Cameron, previously the head gardener at an estate near Dorking, at a salary of £100 per year, together with a rent-free house. Finally, they sought a garden designer. For this they turned to John Claudius Loudon, the foremost landscape gardener, horticulturalist, and garden designer of the early 19th century, and founder and editor of the influential and popular *Gardener's Magazine*. Loudon had married the daughter of a Birmingham manufacturer and had provided David Cameron with a reference for the post of curator. He agreed to provide the design in exchange for just his travel and accommodation expenses. Not surprisingly the committee agreed.

Loudon's proposal extended beyond the plot acquired to include the neighbouring villa occupied by a Mr Apsley, some 16 acres in all.

Loudon was extremely proud of his plans and published them in the *Gardener's Magazine* in August 1832. There was to be a large circular glasshouse for which Loudon provided four alternative designs, depending on how much money was available. From there a straight path descended the slope dissecting the plot in half. There were three ponds with fountains at appropriate junctions with other paths and a 'grand jet' at the bottom. The upper part of the gardens contained serpentine gravelled paths, a rosary, parterres for annual plants, beds of trees, shrubs and perennials, a flower garden, an experimental garden, a flue-heated wall for nectarines and peaches, and an American ground. Below there were more extensive areas for kitchen garden and agricultural crops and for fruit orchards since the committee hoped to raise funds by selling produce raised in the garden.

Loudon's plans for the circular greenhouse were discarded by the committee as too expensive and local manufacturers were asked to quote for a simple metal-framed greenhouse, conservatory and store. The remainder of Loudon's plan was laid out under Cameron's supervision and the gardens opened to the public on 4 June 1832. Loudon was furious that his plans for the circular greenhouse had been abandoned and that much 'nurse' planting of evergreens and beech hedges had been planted

for shelter, against his specific advice. Nonetheless, when he next visited in 1839 he was able to praise the way Cameron had managed the gardens and noted how well trees, shrubs, rhododendrons and azaleas, alpines in pots, and the herbaceous collection 'believed to be the most complete in Britain' were growing. By 1840 the nurse planting was being removed and the orchards were fruiting. Unfortunately, in 1848, the society found themselves unable to keep up with the expenses and negotiated a new lease from the Calthorpe estate for the originally proposed 12 acres and gave up the orchards, the kitchen gardens, the reserve grounds and the heated wall, as well as the site of the grand jet.

The society began holding exhibition shows of flowers and fruits in 1833 and these continued until 1927. There can be no doubt that these shows and the gardens themselves played a large part in the dissemination of new plants and ideas in garden design amongst the middle-class owners of Edgbaston's substantial villas through the 19th century. In the 1870s and '80s work began on replacing and improving the glasshouses. Only one of Loudon's proposed fountains was eventually installed, in 1850, but it was provided by the important Birmingham architectural firm of Charles Edge. He also provided the water-lily

53 The fountain: this was installed in 1850 by Charles Edge.

54 Glasshouses at the Botanical Gardens: the new glasshouses were provided in 1884–5 by subscription.

55 Botanical Gardens, main lawn: a sunny weekend in the 1950s.

56 The Palm House, Botanical Gardens, 1934: the glasshouses were a popular location for society weddings in the inter-war period, as they are today.

house two years later. The attractive lodge building at the entrance was built in the same year to designs by S.S. Teulon. In 1871 a palm house was constructed with a high pyramidal roof. It collapsed in the late 1960s and was rebuilt in a simpler form. The next attraction added was a cast-iron bandstand, built for summer concerts in 1873, by another Birmingham architect, P.B. Osborn. In 1885 the main glasshouses were replaced by those which still exist today. They were completed by Henry Hope at a cost of £4,200 which was raised by subscription. Finally in the 19th century, the rock garden was constructed, towards the bottom of the slope, by Hugh Backhouse & Sons from York in 1894-5. In order to try to increase membership a zoo was added to the attractions in 1910, with bears, monkeys, seals and alligators, together with aviaries of birds. The birds remain today in modern aviaries but the animals had to be given up. A major improvement scheme began in the 1990s with new theme gardens, such as the sunken formal rose garden, and the improvement of existing plantings such as the mid-Victorian fernery. A number of features were moved from elsewhere for preservation, notably a cast-iron gazebo of c.1850 from 32 Church Road. There were also

new attractions, such as the National Collection of Bonsai, housed in a new building. The refurbishment of the glasshouses was an important part of this improvement plan and attached to them was the Pavilion restaurant (1990), which has enabled the Botanical Gardens to enter the profitable hospitality market.

University Botanical Gardens

The university botanical gardens began as the private garden of 'Winterbourne', the house in Edgbaston Park Road that J.S. Nettlefold had built for himself and his family in 1902. The initial garden layout was the responsibility of J.L. Ball, the Arts and Crafts architect of the house, who designed the hard landscaping, and Margaret Nettlefold. Ball designed the extensive kitchen garden (now the rose garden), the grand terraces at the rear of the house, and the long flight of steps leading down the slope. Much of the very large plot of 10 acres was used for a small hobby farm with cows, horses and chickens. Margaret Nettlefold gained her garden inspiration from publications and it is thought that Gertrude Jekyll's book, *Wood and Garden,* was especially influential since it describes a sequence of features very similar to those made at

57   Winterbourne, the entrance front, 1911.

58   The herbaceous border above the rose garden, 1985.

Winterbourne. The elements which still survive include the spectacular rock garden, which was probably installed by the nursery firm of Baker's of Codsall, near Wolverhampton, in 1907; the herringbone brick court, enclosed with yew hedges and containing troughs of alpines; and the spectacular pair of *Wisteria sinensis* which clothe the garden façade of the house. The gardens were maintained by a staff of five, one of whom was responsible for the animals.

J.S. Nettlefold suffered a nervous breakdown in 1914 and, in 1919, Margaret sold the house to a Birmingham stockbroker, Harry Wheelock. He and his wife Edith and their nine children lived there for six years, changing little in the gardens other than using both main lawns for tennis. In 1925 the house was sold to John MacDonald Nicolson, the chairman and managing director of a Birmingham wholesale drapery firm. He and his wife Blanche lived there until his death in 1944. It is to him that we owe many of the features of the garden today, since his overwhelming passion was gardening. In the inter-war years roses and alpine plants were amongst the most fashionable aspects of plantsmanship and Nicolson loved both. He laid out a new rose garden at the east end of the terrace in the form of a series of petals, with alpines edging the beds; he replaced the gravel terrace across the back of the house with crazy paving with rose beds inserted across its breadth; he gave firmer structure to the edge of the upper lawn by planting a row of fastigate Irish yews; and he did the same for the lower lawn by constructing a stone-columned and oak-beamed pergola, another essential feature of a high-quality inter-war garden. In the rock gardens he evoked a Japanese mood by constructing an open-sided tea house and a footbridge over the stream. Beneath the footbridge he had a low dam made to form a pool and

Acers, *Gunnera manicata*, and Skunk cabbage were planted to provide an exotic setting, as they continue to do today, though the bridge is in poor repair. The main alpine area was a large scree bed, with alpine houses and frame, to the north of the crinkle-crankle wall of the kitchen garden. Like his predecessor, he employed four or five gardeners and, on summer Sundays in the 1930s, his garden was regularly open to the public. He managed to continue to maintain the garden through the early years of the war, though the lower field had to be ploughed up for potatoes. He died in 1944 and his ashes are scattered in the garden.

In 1943 Nicolson had decided to bequeath his house and garden to the University of Birmingham 'with the hope that they will maintain it in something like its present form'. Since the university was desperately short of accommodation for the inrush of new students after the war, they used it as a hall of residence annexe to University House, first for 32 women and later, by using all the rooms for students, for 52. The grounds were assigned to the botany department who also acquired a large part of the grounds of the adjoining house, Westmere, for their experimental grounds and glasshouses. Their first major change was in the kitchen garden which was converted to 'Bentham and

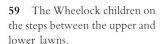
59 The Wheelock children on the steps between the upper and lower lawns.

60 The Nicolsons' grand-daughter with her nanny in the rose garden, 1937.

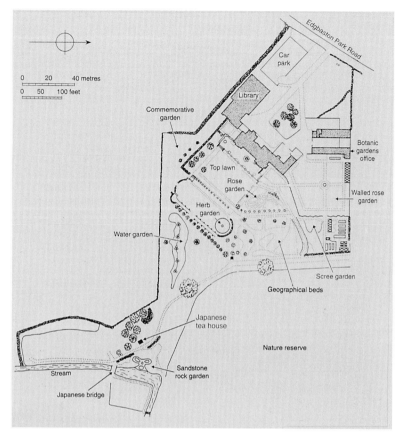

61 Plan of the Botanic Garden, 1989.

Hooker natural order' beds for instructional purposes in taxonomy, though the wall fruits were kept. Next the garden was reduced to just under seven acres as the university sold the lower field to King Edward's Girls School for a playing field. In 1958 Margaret Nettlefold's orchard was grubbed up and replaced by beds of trees and shrubs representative of the Americas, Europe, Australasia and Oriental Asia, and in 1960 a new limestone rock garden, with water-lily pools and a rill, was designed for the area below the pergola. The natural order beds were removed from the walled kitchen garden in the late 1960s to make way for the nationally important collection illustrating the history of rose cultivation in Europe, whilst the small collection of rhododendrons near the rock garden was substantially extended in 1975 to mark the centenary celebrations of Mason College, the forerunner of the university. Finally, a medicinal and culinary herb garden was added at one end of the lower lawn, designed by Dr Richard Lester, and centred on a magnificent ornamental urn derived from the garden wall of Park Grange, in Somerset Road.

Seven

People and Society in the 19th Century

The 1801 census of population tells us that there were 1,155 people resident in Edgbaston. There were a only few more in 1811, but by 1821 the population had increased by more than 75 per cent as the first houses in the Five Ways area and at the bottom of Wellington Road had been constructed. Equally significantly, the proportion of females in the population had increased from 52 to 57 per cent since these new houses were for reasonably prosperous families, most of whom had one or more female servants. The 1831 census was the first to provide a more detailed breakdown of the occupations of residents. Of the, by now, nearly 4,000 people living in the parish, in more than 700 houses (remember there were only 64 a century earlier), we are told that 246 of the males over 20 years of age were 'capitalists, bankers and professionals', 54 were manufacturers, 287 were employed in retail or handicraft, 29 were farmers, 103 were agricultural labourers, 23 were labourers, 77 were servants, and there were 23 unclassified. We are also told that there were 625 female servants in the parish, or a little under one-sixth of the total population, and an average of nearly one for each house in the parish. Since the labourers' households would certainly not have had servants, it is clear that many houses had two or more, and the best houses would also have had a gardener and a groom to look after the carriages and horses.

Edgbaston's population increased steadily with each decade of the 19th century, usually by between two and four thousand people, but the percentage increase reduced steadily, of course, from the peak of nearly 87 per cent in 1831 to only 7.4 per cent in 1891. The proportion of women also increased slowly to a peak of 61.4 per cent in 1871. Thereafter it remained at roughly the same proportion until after the First World War, when a combination of labour-saving domestic devices and higher wages meant that far fewer households were able to afford servants. In the 19th century most servants worked for 14 hours a day or more and had only one day off a month. The

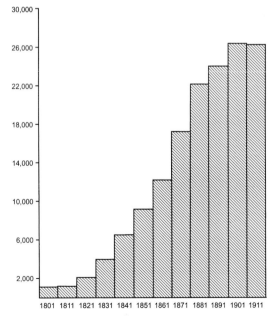

62 Edgbaston's population increases in the 19th century.

Date	Population	% Increase	Males	Females	% Females
1801	1,155	—	550	605	52.4
1811	1,180	2.2	537	643	54.5
1821	2,117	79.4	908	1,209	57.1
1831	3,954	86.8	1,653	2,301	58.2
1841	6,609	67.1	2,660	3,949	59.8
1851	9,269	40.3	3,676	5,593	60.3
1861	12,907	39.3	5,017	7,890	61.1
1871	17,442	35.1	6,728	10,714	61.4
1881	22,760	30.5	8,981	13,779	60.5
1891	24,436	7.4	9,468	14,968	61.3
1901	26,486	8.4	10,327	16,159	61.0
1911	26,398	0.3	10,099	16,299	61.7

Table 2.   Edgbaston Population 1801–1911.

Parish	Area	Houses	Uninhab.	Building	Population	Males	Females
St Barthol.	2021 ac.	1073	47	25	6469	2415	4054
St George	258 ac.	967	19	16	5355	1948	3407
St James	150 ac.	1086	37	16	5618	2365	3253

Table 3.   Houses and Population by Ecclesiastical Parish, 1871.

vast majority were in the 16–30 age group, came from Birmingham or the surrounding villages, and went into service as a prelude to marriage in their late 20s or 30s.

Local newspapers were always full of advertisements for servants, though most house-holders would have preferred personal recom-mendations. Thus the *Birmingham Daily Post* carried an advertisement, in October 1864, for 'a good general servant. She must be sober, honest, industrious and of good character. Apply this (Tuesday) morning at No. 1 The Hawthorns, Gough Road, Edgbaston'. Given their long working day, almost all these servants 'lived in', having small spartan rooms in the attics of the house or, in the case of grooms and gardeners, over the stables or in the gate lodge. Most female servants were categorised as 'general' servants, or housemaids, who could be asked to do almost anything. Rather more specialised and superior in status were cooks and nannies, and they also had better accom-modation though, in the latter case, often

sharing with the children and therefore lacking privacy.

Using the enumerator's returns of the 1881 census as an example, we get the opportunity to look a little more closely into some Edgbaston households. If we begin with the three large mansions to the south of Edgbaston Park, 'Park Vale', 'Park Mount' and 'Park Grove', all fronting on to the Bristol Road, we find that 'Park Vale' was then occupied by George Taylor and his family. Taylor was a scion of the family in partnership with the Lloyds, together forming Birmingham's first private bank. However, Taylor had not been attracted to banking and had become a brewer. Though aged 77, he was still active as a brewer and maltster and employed 21 people in his brewery. Sarah, his wife, was much younger at 64, and their two adult children, also Sarah (aged 41) and George (aged 29), lived with them. They had three female servants, Hannah Parkes, Annie Bayliss and Amelia Smith, all Birmingham-born women and aged 32, 22 and 20 respectively. At 'Park

Mount', Edward Udal was a 30-year-old brass merchant living with his unmarried sister Jane (25). They, too, had three female servants, this time specified as housekeeper (Jane Hayward, aged 47), cook (Sarah Slinn, aged 50), and housemaid (Mary Preston, aged 25). However, there was also Gabriel Watts and his large family living in the lodge. Gabriel was the gardener and was assisted by his 16-year-old son, Harry. They had five children in total, the youngest of whom was 10, and all lived in the little lodge which still stands on the Bristol Road. Finally, in 'Park Grove' was John Jaffray, newspaper proprietor, and his wife Anna, both 62 years old. They had a cook, Sarah Gatehouse (51), a housemaid, Maria Bishop (38), a kitchenmaid, Mary Hewitt (20), and, unusually, a footman Thomas White (27). As at 'Park Mount', the lodge was occupied by the gardener, George Alcock (48), his wife Mary, described as lodge keeper, and their three sons, George, John and William. George, at 16, had already found employment at Jaffray's newspaper office as a printer compositor. The women servants had probably been with the Jaffrays for many years as they are rather older than most servants, and the Alcocks had occupied the lodge all their married life, since the children had all been born there.

The reality of large numbers of young children in élite households is well shown by Dr Ludwig Denmuth (43), a German-born manufacturing chemist, and his Manchester-born wife Hannah (38), who occupied 'Wharfedale' in Church Road. Hannah had given birth to eight children over the previous 12 years (four boys and four girls) and so there was a governess to look after them, as well as a cook, a kitchenmaid, two housemaids, and three domestic servants, besides Hannah's unmarried 25-year-old sister. Nearby, in 'Edgbaston Grove' lived George Lloyd (56), retired banker, alderman of the city, and magistrate, and his wife Mary and son, John (25), already in business as an iron tube manufacturer. Two young cousins of George, aged

9 and 10, lived with them, the likelihood being that he was their guardian. There were four servants, specified as cook, parlour maid, serving maid and domestic servant, the only unusual feature being the age of Helen Preston, the cook, who was only 25. However, the lodge housed the Hogg family, Alexander and Emma and their three sons. The whole family provided five more employees for the Lloyds since they are specified as three gardeners and two grooms. Twenty years earlier, in 1861, Lloyd and his then young family were living at 23 Wellington Road and had three servants (a cook and two housemaids). George B. Lloyd II was a member of the Quaker Lloyd's banking family. He was the younger of two brothers and had therefore set up his own company, G.B. Lloyd and Co., boiler tube manufacturers, in Gas Street (hence his son's occupation in 1881). However, on his father's death in 1857 he joined his brother as a partner in Lloyd's Bank and helped steer it to joint-stock status in 1865. Since the demand for shares was high, he became an extremely rich man.

63 The lodge, 'Edgbaston Grove': George Lloyd's house has been demolished but the lodge remains. The Hogg family lived here in 1881 as gardeners and grooms.

64 One of the smaller houses in the lower part of Wellington Road. The magnificent Chile pine, or Monkey Puzzle tree, was fashionable in the late 19th century and may have been purchased from George and Sarah Nicholls' nursery.

If we now look in the smaller, older houses towards the middle and bottom of Wellington Road in 1881, we find that there are fewer servants and the households are much more varied. At No. 42 lived John Millward (74) and his wife Isabella (82), together with their youngest unmarried daughter Caroline (34) and an elderly lodger, Martha Leake (85) who lived on an annuity, a not unusual situation for members of the middle classes in the 19th century. They had only a cook and a young servant, Fanny Forrester (16), to look after them. Caroline had probably despaired of ever marrying and was helping to look after the rest of this elderly household. Yet Millward was a well-to-do manufacturer of weighing machines with a workforce of almost 90 employees in

his factory. He presumably still managed it since he is not described as retired. As with Lloyd, we find him in 1861 already living in Wellington Road, when his house is described as 'The Firs', which enables us to locate it on the north-west corner of the junction with Carpenter Road. We also discover that John and Isabella had had five children in quick succession since they were aged 14-19 in 1861. They had only a cook and housemaid in 1861 too, so he seems to have been a man who watched his pennies carefully!

At No. 44 was William Robbins (53), a retired teacher of dancing, and his wife Sarah (42), making do with only one general servant. Next door was Edward Wright, a manufacturing engineer, again with a large factory employing nearly 190 men and boys. He and wife Elizabeth and daughter Ellen (19) had only a cook and housemaid. At No. 46, two small cottages, described as Lees Farm in 1861, were occupied by gardeners and, again, both families are found at the same address in 1861. John Jones was 76 in 1881 and was a jobbing gardener for nearby houses. In 1861 he and wife Sarah had had a young schoolboy, Robert Cuttler (aged 6), boarding with them. In the other cottage Sarah Nicholls (53), already widowed in 1881, and her middle son William (24) were running a commercial enterprise, since they are described as florist gardeners. Third son, Herbert, was a clerk in the county court in Birmingham, and there were two younger daughters living there as well. In 1861 we discover that Sarah's husband had been called George and was only three years older than her. Their daughters had not been born then, but the boys were young, so there was an assistant gardener George Page, who lodged with them, and a young girl, Ann Gordon, aged 12, to help Sarah in the house.

By contrast with Wellington Road, the houses in Balsall Heath Road were very much lower middle-class/skilled working-class in status, but were more modern and still quite substantial houses. At one end of the street, at No. 72, was the no-doubt upwardly mobile

Benjamin Blissett (35), a hardware merchant, his wife Clara (28) and young daughter Mabel (3), complete with cook and maid. Next door, at No. 74, was the even more successful John Whittles, only 39, but already described as a retired chemist. His wife Mary (35) had borne him four children, Walter (12), Sidney (11), Florence (9) and Blanche (7), and Whittles had engaged Emma Piper (24) as governess. They also employed brother and sister George and Elizabeth Morton as groom and general servant respectively, but there was no cook. However, at the other end of the street, No. 24 was occupied by Joseph Reece (48), an engine and machine fitter, his wife Sarah (54), and their five children with ages ranging from 12 to 26, but there were no servants. At No. 26 lived William Brown (66), a house painter, his wife Eliza (62) and unmarried daughter, also Eliza (37), and, again, no servants. Finally, at No. 27 widow Rebecca Bailey (aged 80) took in lodgers, Sarah Blackford and Mary Ward (25), a shop assistant, to make ends meet.

If we return to Wellington Road, but to 1861 rather than 1881, it is noticeable that families were generally much larger and more fluid, with relatives of various descriptions living with the main family. Merchant Samuel Booth and his wife Mary, at No. 50, had both Mary's elderly mother and four teenage nieces and nephews living with them. Samuel was presumably their guardian since they are not described as visitors. Four servants, including a 12-year-old pageboy, looked after them. John Webster, at No. 47, had his wife's aunt living with them and their three sons, whilst Norland House was occupied by an especially complex household: two middle-aged Irish women, both described as clergymen's wives, were living with the six children of one (aged 6-26) and the young niece of the other, together with four servants, one of whom was described as nurse. Especially affecting is the record of the family at Dorset House where William James (40), a screw manufacturer, had recently lost his wife in childbirth. His young family, Edward (4),

Mary (3), Agnes (1) and Frances (two months) were being looked after by two nurse-maids, and there was a cook and housemaid too.

Wellington Road also demonstrates the social mix of occupations in Edgbaston at this time. At the bottom of the social scale were the gardeners, coachmen and house-keepers occupying the lodges to the larger mansions. There was also a Chelsea pensioner living in the road. Next come the lower rank professionals: a police officer (there was a police station at the bottom of the road), a commercial traveller, agents for Norwich Union and a local firm of carriers, and a pawnbroker, Salman Sachs (78), one of the oldest members of Edgbaston's Jewish community; the secretaries of the Birmingham Fire Office and the Birmingham Waterworks probably belong here, too, as does the accountant/cashier, the optician and the retired dentist. Other professionals include a school principal, the curate of Edgbaston church, three attorneys, and the banker whom we have already met. Two members of the town council lived in the road and four people lived on invested income. There were seven manufacturers: two gunmakers, two screw manufacturers, an electro-plater, a clockmaker, and a 'merchant manufacturer'. Several of them employed 100 people or more. Finally, there were the merchants and wholesalers dealing in such things as iron, paper, hops and seeds, tea, provisions and linen, ten in total and many of them making an extremely good living.

The most prominent members of Birmingham's Jewish community lived in Edgbaston when they could afford to do so because it was within walking distance from the Singer's Hill synagogue. Salman Sachs and Abraham Newich, the president of the Singer's Hill congregation in the 1840s, who lived in George Road, were the first residents, but by 1871 there were at least eighty families living in the suburb in three geographical groupings. The lowest status group was that centred on Belgrave Road to the east of Bristol Road; a second group was nearby on Bristol Road and

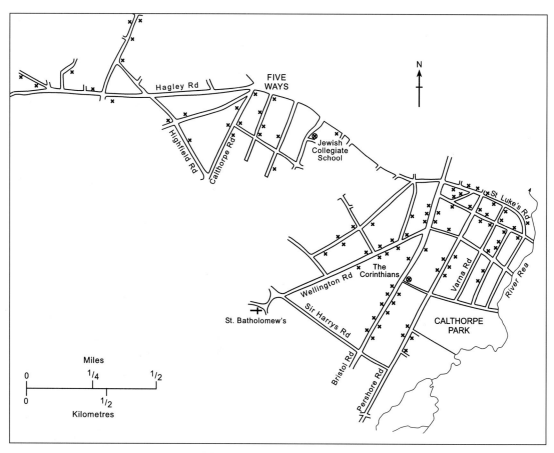

65   Edgbaston's Jewish community in 1871.

Wellington Road, but of higher status; and a third, more dispersed, group lived in the Frederick Road, Calthorpe Road and Hagley Road area. The most notable Jewish household in the later 19th century was that of Michal Davis at 'The Corinthians' on the corner of Speedwell Road and Bristol Road, which still stands. It had what was regarded as the largest room in Edgbaston for his Friday Sabbath gathering, and a permanent Succah, a booth open to the sky to celebrate harvest festival, though in this case the glass roof was raised by a winch. The house also gave name to the athletic club of the same name which had playing fields on Pershore Road provided by the Birmingham Athletic Institute. Lawrence Levy, who we shall meet in a later chapter,

was a prominent athlete in his younger days and later founded the Jewish Collegiate School in Wheeley's Road. It is thanks to his published reminiscences that we know that playing cards, especially whist, was one of the great social activities in the community in the 1870s, and that weddings and dances usually took place at the *Plough and Harrow* on Hagley Road, until the Edgbaston Assembly Rooms opened.

Most social intercourse in Edgbaston took place in the domestic setting of the home and, until the later 19th century, there were few other gathering places. Church services on Sundays provided the opportunity for conversation, though for many non-Anglican residents, including Unitarians, Quakers and Catholics, services meant a journey into Birmingham. For much of the century these denominational distinctions were just as significant as that between Jew and Christian, and there was certainly not just one upper-middle-class ethos in the suburb. The *Plough and Harrow* provided the only other meeting place and processions at the laying of foundation stones, or the opening of new churches, for example, usually began and ended there with gargantuan feasts and toast-making. The luxuriously appointed

Edgbaston Assembly Rooms, on the corner of Francis Road and Hagley Road, was therefore an important addition to the social facilities. It opened in 1884, to designs by Messrs Osborn and Reading, and operated as a commercial company. It provided several suites of rooms that could be used separately or as a single complex for meetings, balls, wedding receptions, concerts and drama productions. The main room could accommodate up to 700

66 The *Plough and Harrow* hotel on Hagley Road was the main centre for social gatherings until the 1880s.

67 The Drawing Room, No. 21 Yateley Road: this exotic Art Nouveau interior is not typical of Edgbaston interiors but demonstrates well the often crowded furnishings.

68   The Ballroom of Edgbaston Assembly Rooms, *c*.1884.

69   Lt H. James VC.

people and basement kitchens could provide food for that number. The first event was a dinner for the Birmingham Law Society.

From 1881 *Edgbastonia* began its forty-year career of turgid writing, as the free magazine delivered to quality houses in Edgbaston. It contains remarkably little local news, its principal feature being a monthly biographical sketch of prominent Edgbastonians alive (usually just!) or dead. During the First World War the obituary notices of young officers killed at the Front were another feature of the magazine, but it took most of the war before anything other than patriotic fervour found expression as the sons of Edgbaston's families fell in swathes. The proudest moment came in 1915 when Lt H. James, from unfashionable Poplar Road, was awarded the Victoria Cross for gallantry at Gallipoli. Amazingly he lived to tell the tale!

Eight

Edgbaston Churches

Edgbaston parish church, St Bartholomew's, has been known for nearly two centuries as Edgbaston old church. It was first documented in 1279, when it was still a chapel of Harborne, and consisted of a nave and small chancel. Like many medieval chapels it was probably built by the lord of the manor for his own use and that of his retainers on the estate, and so stands close to the manor house. The south porch was the main entrance, facing the hall and linked to it by a path. A north aisle was added in the late 15th century by Richard Middlemore, the then lord of the manor, probably as a funerary chapel for the family, whilst his widow added the low pinnacled west tower in 1503. The church was badly damaged during the Civil War as we have seen, when it was seized in 1643, along with the Hall, by Parliamentarian Colonel 'Tinker' Fox. Lead from the roof was melted to make bullets, timbers used to barricade the Hall, and horses stabled in the nave. The bells were sold and the monuments defaced or destroyed. When Sir William Dugdale came to write about the church for his *Antiquities of Warwickshire Illustrated* a few years later, he had to use memories of the monuments in his description, but he was able to describe the heraldry in the stained glass of some of the windows. He described the church as 'utterly demolished', but clearly the walls were still standing. Beside the churchyard was the 'Little House standing called the Schoole house, or the Priest's Chamber, which is now totally burnt and consumed in the late time of the Warr', whereas the 'old House called Antiently

by the name of the Church House, in which the Parrish have usually mett about Parochiall Affaires ... adjoining to the Church Yard' seems to have survived. Consequently, extensive repairs were required when the uncertainties of the war had subsided.

Ten years later, in 1658, the parishioners gained permission to make a collection amongst neighbouring parishes and throughout the west midland counties to fund the rebuilding. Another brief was issued in 1684 for the same purpose, so it must be assumed that the rebuilding was spread over much of the later 17th century. Though the tower was still standing, its upper stages had to be taken down and rebuilt. A sundial was added to the south wall of the tower, and the refurbishment also included interior pewing in the 17th-century fashion. When Sir Richard Gough became lord of the manor he ensured that any remaining repair work was completed, augmented the value of the living to £200 per annum, acquired the advowson of the living from the Dean and Chapter of Lichfield for himself and his heirs, and reorganised the pews. A comparative 'before and after' plan of the interior of the church in 1721 survives from this reorganisation. We can therefore see that a smaller communion table and new rails seem to have been provided in the chancel, that the font stood against the pillar between the north and south doors, that the pulpit was half-way along the south wall, and that Sir Richard built himself a large box pew half-way down the north side of the nave, facing

70 Edgbaston old church, 1793: drawn by William Hamper for his annotated and extra-illustrated copy of Dugdale's *History of Warwickshire Illustrated*, this shows the north side just before the church was re-roofed.

71 Edgbaston old church, 1812: this painting shows the east end following the re-roofing of the church under a single span.

72 Edgbaston old church, 1829: as Edgbaston's population increased the churchyard filled rapidly and had to be extended.

the pulpit. The reorganisation of the remaining pews meant that the benches for the poorer people of the parish had to be removed from the back of the nave and aisle, and only a little standing room was left at the back of the church. There were no further alterations in the 18th century and we have several illustrations of the exterior of the church at this time.

By 1800 the central valley between the two roofs was a great source of trouble and frequently leaked into the church, whilst there was a pressing need for more seating as the population of the parish was growing, and so, in 1810, it was decided to re-roof the church under a single span and add a gallery. The old roofs and the interior pillars were removed, some of the windows were replaced with cast-iron frames, the walls were raised, and a broad new roof constructed over the whole. It had a classical cornice around the outside, ending in a pediment-like termination at the east end, and a flat plaster ceiling inside, all completely at odds with the gothic character of the older structure. Probably at the same time, the south door was stopped up to make room for a stove to provide heating, with a new churchwarden's pew beside it! A narrow west gallery was added to increase the seating and a small vestry and staircase were built in the south-west corner beside the tower.

The increasing population of the parish meant not only a need for more congregational space for the living, but also a larger churchyard for the dead, and so the churchyard was enlarged in 1836 by taking in the rickyard of the home farm to the west. In 1845 antiquarian sensibilities were recognised and the cast-iron windows were replaced by stone tracery ones, the exterior walls raised again, and the church re-roofed again, all making room for a much larger interior gallery to increase the seating accommodation. Eleven years later, in 1856, the church was enlarged still further by the addition of a south aisle to the designs of J.A. Cossins, together with a new vestry beside the north wall of the chancel.

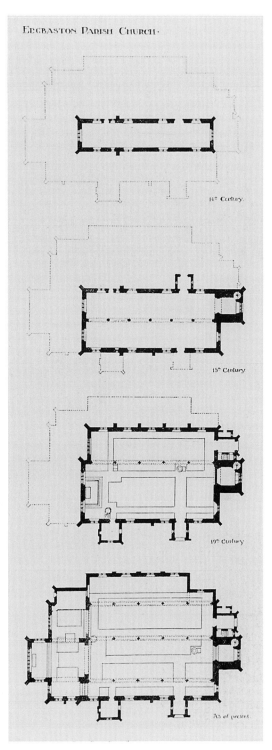

73 Plans of the successive enlargement of Edgbaston old church.

74   Edgbaston old church choir, *c.*1930.

The arrival of Rev. Cresswell Strange as vicar in 1885 saw another phase of rebuilding. A new enlarged chancel and chancel aisles extended the church to the east and, since this was intended to Gothicise the building by moving the altar to the central axis, a new arcade was inserted to form a north aisle, whilst the south aisle was extended to provide more seating. All this was funded by the Middlemore brothers, William, Richard and James. J.A. Chatwin was the architect for these alterations and he provided designs for new choir pews, reredos, pulpit and other furnishings, as well as the splendid timber roofs. Most of the stained glass windows in the church also date from the second half of the 19th century and are from the studio of John Hardman. The fine William Hill organ was installed in 1857, and was rebuilt and enlarged in 1890. The peal of eight bells were recast in 1927 but contain four of the oldest bells in the diocese, cast in 1685 by the Bagley brothers. The 20th century has seen the addition of a parish room at the west end of the church in the 1960s and the refurbishment of the vestry in 1977. It has also seen the addition of two notable art works: a 'Madonna and Child'

thought to be by Eric Gill which came from St James's Church on its closure; and a new millennium high altar frontal and cope by Juliet Hemingray of Derby, Britain's foremost ecclesiastical textile designer. St Bartholomew's vast neo-Gothic Victorian vicarage was an impressive house, even by Edgbaston standards, but, inevitably, was replaced by a modern house in the 1960s. The churchyard contains the remains of many of Birmingham's most notable 19th-century citizens resident in Edgbaston.

St George's Church
As a result of the late 19th-century rebuilding, the old church could seat 600 parishioners, a relatively small number by Birmingham parish standards, but other parish churches had by then been built in Edgbaston. St George's Church, in Calthorpe Road, was built originally in 1836-8, to designs in an Early English style by J.J. Scoles, on land donated by George, 3rd Lord Calthorpe (hence the dedication), who also provided most of the £6,000 which it cost to build. Both the laying of the foundation stone and the dedication of the church were accompanied by lavish ceremonial, feasting

(at the *Plough and Harrow*) and the drinking of toasts. The new church seated almost one thousand. It acquired its own parish from St Bartholomew's in 1852. A chancel (now the lady chapel) and vestry was added to the existing nave in 1856, and a low spire with a clock and bell built in the north-east angle of the church, all to designs by Charles Edge. As at the old church, it was the coming of a new vicar in 1883, the Rev. Charles Owen, which set in train a massive extension and refurbishment of St George's in 1884-5, and once more it was to designs by J.A. Chatwin, at a cost of £6,000. It involved the demolition of the south aisle of the original church and the building of a new nave, chancel, south aisle and choir vestry which more than trebled the size of the church. The plan also envisaged a tower and spire over the choir vestry, but this was never built. Choir stalls, organ and mosaic pavement in the chancel were added subsequently, as were a number of stained

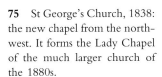

75 St George's Church, 1838: the new chapel from the north-west. It forms the Lady Chapel of the much larger church of the 1880s.

76 St George's Church, *c*.1880: the church was massively increased in size to designs by J.A. Chatwin.

77 St George's Church: this engraving appeared in *Edgbastonia* in 1884 and shows the proposed tower and spire which was never completed.

78 St George's proposed vicarage, 1897: vicars were important members of the community and lived in houses the equal of those of their parishioners.

glass windows, some by the Hardman studio in Birmingham, but others by London firms, whilst the east window of the Lady Chapel is by Kempe. The magnificent oak reredos dates from 1903-4 and was carved by Bridgeman of Lichfield, to the designs of P.B. Chatwin; the original intention was that it should be painted by the Bromsgove Guild, but this was never carried out. The church was damaged by a wartime bomb and, sadly, lost the railings which surrounded the churchyard to the war effort. It is currently in the midst of a major restoration to replace the roofs and rainwater goods.

Other Parish Churches

St James's Church, in Charlotte Road, was built in 1852, at the same time as St George's was created a parish. Frederick, 4th Lord Calthorpe, paid for the building which is in Decorated Gothic style, designed by S.S. Teulon, at a cost of £3,000. Teulon also designed the new Elvetham Hall in Hampshire for the Calthorpes. St James's is a cruciform building with a low tower in the south-west angle and stands prominently on rising ground. The stained glass east window was added in 1887. There were 700 free sittings and St James's was assigned a parish from St Bartholomew's immediately in 1852.

It was made redundant in 1975 and for some years was used by the Bible Society as a training college.

St Augustine's Church, in Lyttleton (St Augustine's) Road, was built in 1868 at a cost of £9,000 to 13th-century Gothic designs by, again, J.A. Chatwin. The dramatic tall tower and spire on the south side, some 185 feet high, was added in 1876 for a further £4,000; Pevsner considered the proportions 'really horrid'! It was built to serve the houses being built on the Gillott estate, to the north of the Hagley Road, and Gillott provided the site. For some decades it stood alone in the fields as house-building spread towards it and it may be for this reason that it was not created a parish until 1889. Part of the parish was transferred to St John's, Harborne in 1906, and part to form St Germain's, Edgbaston in 1920. Its vicar in the first decade of the 20th century, Winfrid Burrows, was the first Archdeacon of Birming-

ham and went on to become Bishop of Truro and then of Chichester. Like St George's, St Augustine's had a strong musical tradition in the 1880-1914 period.

SS Mary and Ambrose church, on the Pershore Road, began life as one of two mission churches of St Bartholomew's in 1886. The 'tin tabernacle' parish hall was purchased from St Agnes, Moseley, where it had served as that parish's first church building. A school room was added and then a permanent church constructed in 1897-8. The parish was created in 1903. The site was given by the 6th Lord Calthorpe and the building, designed by J.A. Chatwin, cost £12,000. Its rich red-brick and terracotta structure is a prominent part of the view from Edgbaston County Cricket Ground. The oak screen was erected as a First World War memorial in 1921, and three baptistery windows are a memorial to Canon Strange, the first vicar.

79 St James's Church from Charlotte Road, c.1935.

St Germain's Church stands on the corner of Portland and City Roads and is one of only two churches in England erected during the course of the First World War. Technically it is not within the ancient parish of Edgbaston, but since it was carved out of St Augustine's it is included here. The dedication had originally been to St German but popular protest in the context of the war determined a change. It was

built between 1915 and 1917, in an unusual brick Byzantine style, with an apsidal east end and ambulatory, to designs by the important Birmingham Arts and Crafts architect Edwin Reynolds, FRIBA. Despite the war it is built of rich materials with Swedish green marble columns around the apse. The internal decorative scheme was never completed, however. Reynolds intended that the massive truss and

80   *Left.* The 'tin tabernacle' that preceded SS Mary and Ambrose.

81   *Below left.* St Mary and St Ambrose: this drawing of Chatwin's design for a new church on the Pershore Road embellished the appeal leaflet for its building.

82   *Below right.* St Augustine's Church from the south-west, *c.*1913: the circus of Lyttleton Road was still not built up.

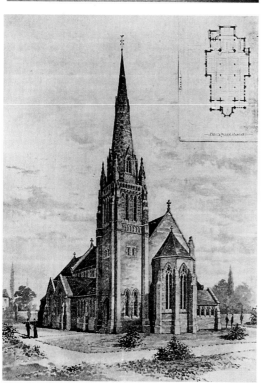

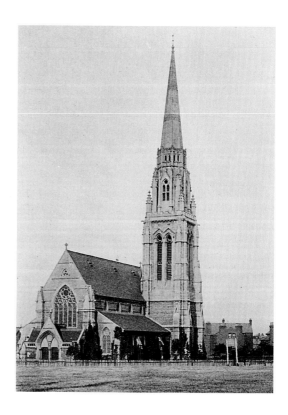

83 *Right.* St Germain's Church, *c.*1935.

84 *Below right.* Interior of St Germain's Church, *c.*1935

purlin roof timbers should be pattern-painted, that the walls should be frescoed, the chancel walls panelled with marble, and the semi-dome covered with a mosaic. The attractive contemporary vicarage stands beside it, together with a modern parish hall, which succeeded the iron mission church first erected by Christ Church, Summerfield in 1896. The mission was transferred to St Augustine's in 1906 and became an independent parish in 1920. As with all Edgbaston's churches, St Germain's had a large number of active social groups. Particularly important for encouraging the membership of young people were the uniformed organisations that have their origins in the late 19th or early 20th century at the height of Empire. The most successful of these organisations were the Boy Scouts and Girl Guides founded by Lord and Lady Baden-Powell. The St Germain's Scout Group was one of the earliest in Birmingham, being founded only five years after the movement was created in 1907. The Group Scout Leader in the inter-war period, Mr Tommy Parkes, ran the group with enthusiasm and discipline, and its band was well-known throughout the parish as it led the group to church parades. The group had its own scout hut in Portland Road.

It can be seen that two of these parish churches derived from mission buildings planting new congregations in new housing areas or working-class districts. There were other missions that did not develop into parishes. The longest-lived was St Monica's, in Harrison's Road, built in 1891 by the old church and closed only in the mid-1960s. St George's had a mission in Parker Street between 1904 and 1914 which was succeeded by St George's Institute in Waterworks Road, which survived until 1968. St Augustine's sponsored three mission chapels in its long, narrow parish between 1891 and 1918, but all were short-lived.

Nonconformity

There were few nonconformist churches in Edgbaston because of the difficulty of obtaining sites from the Anglican Calthorpes. All served either the Gillott estate north of the Hagley Road, or in one case the terraced streets around Calthorpe Park. The most prominent building was the Baptist Church of the Redeemer, formerly in Hagley Road, which was built in 1881-2 at a cost of £25,000, to designs by James Cubitt, on a site provided by W. Middlemore. It seated 1,000 people, and though there was a congregation of only 276 at its foundation this had doubled by 1909. It was a tall, cruciform, Gothic building with galleries inside. It had a distinctive central lantern tower that was a prominent landmark on Hagley Road. Its tall pinnacles and parapet had to be taken down for safety reasons, and the whole church was demolished in the mid-1970s and replaced with a small modern building in Monument Road. A second Baptist congregation was formed on Balsall Heath Road and in 1900 it moved into a

new church in Edward Road facing Calthorpe Park. Another prominent church, in Francis Road, belonged to the Congregationalists. This was built in 1856 and substantially enlarged in 1892-3. The building was cruciform, in Early English style, with a tall spire at the west end, and was designed by Yeoville Thomason. It originated as a mission from Carrs Lane church in the city centre. Finally there is the Wesleyan Methodist complex in Sandon Road, at the Bearwood end of Edgbaston. The first chapel here was opened in 1882. This was replaced in 1890 by a larger building and further enlargement took place in 1904. As well as the church there was a complex of seven rooms, which included a Sunday school hall.

85 St Germain's vicarage living room, *c.*1935: this photograph of the vicar was taken for the 25th anniversary celebrations.

86 74th Birmingham (St Germain's) Scout Group and Guide Company, 1962.

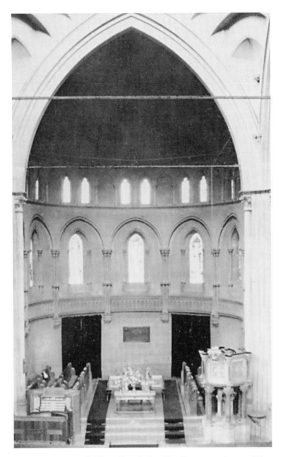

87 Interior of Church of the Redeemer: the stubby cruciform plan of the Redeemer was fitted with galleries to hold a large congregation.

88 Edgbaston Friends' Meeting House, George Road: the Quaker Meeting was established here in 1893 from Broad Street.

The Birmingham Oratory

The Roman Catholic Church of St Philip Neri at the Oratory on the Hagley Road originated as the chapel which served the Oratory community founded by John Henry Newman in 1852 and so re-established the long Catholic tradition in Edgbaston. Rebuilding of the chapel began in 1903 and was completed in 1909, to designs by E. Doran Webb as a memorial to Cardinal Newman at a cost of £40,000. It is a basilica in Italian Renaissance style and is dominated externally by its copper dome and, internally, by the huge 18 ft. high Corinthian pillars of Serravezza marble. These were shipped from Italy, two at a time, by steamer, and then by canal to the Monument Road wharf. The fine mosaics in the sanctuary and elsewhere were made in Murano, Venice, and the altar came from a church in Rome. There are domestic premises for the Brothers of the Order attached to the church in Florentine Renaissance style, which were built to designs by Henry Clutton in 1852. There was also, from the beginning, a boys school whose pupils included J.R.R. Tolkien and Hilaire Belloc. Newman, who was born in 1801, was a theologian of high renown, as well as a fine novelist and poet. He was elected a Fellow of Oriel College, Oxford in 1822 and ordained priest two years later. In 1828 he became vicar of St Mary's, the

89 *Top.* Exterior of the Oratory: the Oratory church's exterior can only be seen from the playground of St Philip's school.

90 *Above.* Cardinal Newman: Newman was one of Edgbaston's most famous residents in the late 19th century.

university church, where he became one of the leaders of the so-called 'Oxford Movement', which sought to reintroduce many of the forms and tenets of Roman Catholic worship and theology into Anglicanism. His spiritual journey ultimately led him to leave the Church of England and be received into the Roman Catholic Church in 1845. For a period he stayed at Oscott College in Erdington and then went to Rome where he was priested in 1847. He returned with the Pope's permission to establish an English oratory in Birmingham which was founded in Alcester Street in 1849. The London Brompton Oratory was founded a few months later. By 1852 the Birmingham institution had been removed to Hagley Road and Newman lived there until his death in 1890 (except for the years 1854-8). It was here that he wrote 'The Dream of Gerontius' in 1865, here that he received the news that he had been created Cardinal in 1879, and here that his portrait was painted by Millais in 1881. His rooms in the Oratory have been preserved as he left them.

Nine

Getting Around the Suburb:
Transport Improvements

In the 18th century the rapidly developing industries of Birmingham created a demand for better transport facilities to enable raw materials to be brought into the town and to allow finished products to be transported to their markets. Increasingly those markets were not just regional but national and even international. From the mid-17th century, when roads had been the responsibility of the parishes through which they passed, whether they were local roads or important long-distance routes, the principal means of improving them had been the turnpike trust. Such trusts were empowered to finance the improvement of road surfaces and drainage, the construction of new lengths of road, and the construction and maintenance of bridges, by levying tolls on the users of the roads. In the 18th century, toll-gates, and their attendant's lodge cottage, became a familiar sight alongside main roads.

There were three such roads in Edgbaston. First was the road to Bromsgrove, Worcester and Bristol turnpiked in 1725-6. From medieval times this route had left Birmingham via Edgbaston Street, up Holloway Head, to Bath Row, then via Wheeley's Road, Arthur Road and down Priory Road. From there it cut across from the corner of Edgbaston Park to the Over Mill below the pool, and so to the bottom of Edgbaston Park Road. The toll-house and gate were at the top of Priory Road, near the entrance to the Park. The present broad straight stretch of the Bristol Road, from Bristol Street

91 The old turnpike gate at the top of Edgbaston Park Road, 1730.

(then called Exeter Street) to the 'Gun Barrels' in Bournbrook, was not created until 1771. The old road past the mill was abandoned and a new toll-gate was built where Priory Road crossed the new road.

The new Bristol Road was paralleled by a completely new turnpike road to Pershore in 1825 which cut across the meadowlands beside the River Rea. It had a toll-gate and cottage near to Pebble Mill, which by the mid-19th century was an elegant two-storey Victorian Gothic cottage with elegantly carved barge boards and multi-colour brickwork. On the north side of the parish, Grindlestone Lane, which was to become the Hagley Road, was turnpiked in 1753. It had toll-gates at the top end of Islington Row and Broad Street at Five Ways, and also at the junction with Sandon Road, at what was called 'the two-mile stump', which was the road to Smethwick.

All these roads were heavily used by local manufacturers. From the early 19th century they were also used by horse-drawn bus companies to provide a service for the increasing numbers of people choosing to leave the crowded streets of Birmingham and take up residence in new suburbs. Turnpikes, buses and builders enjoyed a symbiotic relationship around all Britain's large cities in the early 19th century, and Birmingham was no exception. However, in Edgbaston, thanks to the near monopoly in the supply of land enjoyed by the Calthorpes, it was the surrounding village centres that began to develop quickly with the smaller cottage properties favoured by those who needed the

92   Edgbaston turnpike gate, Bristol Road, *c.*1830.

93   Pershore Road turnpike cottage, Pebble Mill.

94   Horse-drawn bus on Hagley Road, *c*.1885.

services of the bus operators to get them to work each day and home again in the evening. Harborne, Bearwood, Selly Oak and Bournbrook were the destinations of the six or more horse-buses a day that began to traverse each of the turnpikes and the road to Harborne from the 1830s onwards. By the 1870s these services had increased substantially, to provide a half-hourly service to each of the now rapidly growing suburbs.

Birmingham and Worcester Canal

Important though new and improved roads were for the local economy, heavier manufactured goods, together with the all-important coal to fuel the new steam-powered factories from the 1780s onwards, needed water transport. Because of its notable lack of navigable rivers, Birmingham's industrialists were in the forefront of the campaign to develop canal links from the mid-18th century. As a consequence Birmingham was to develop into the hub of

the English canal network. Edgbaston's part in this was to provide the south-west 'spoke' of the network, to the River Severn at Worcester and thereby onwards to Gloucester and Bristol. The Birmingham and Worcester Canal Act was passed in 1791 authorising the construction of the canal. Since the surveyed route was across the Edgbaston estate of the Calthorpes, Sir Henry Gough-Calthorpe took the precaution of becoming an investor and shareholder in the company. He also ensured that when the Bill was passing through Parliament clauses were inserted which prohibited the construction of any industrial buildings along its length through the parish and ensured that the towpath was on the opposite side of the canal to the hall and park.

The construction of the canal took a considerable time as a long tunnel had to be built at Kings Norton, and a very long flight of locks was required to descend from the Birmingham Plateau at Tardebigge. The canal was finally

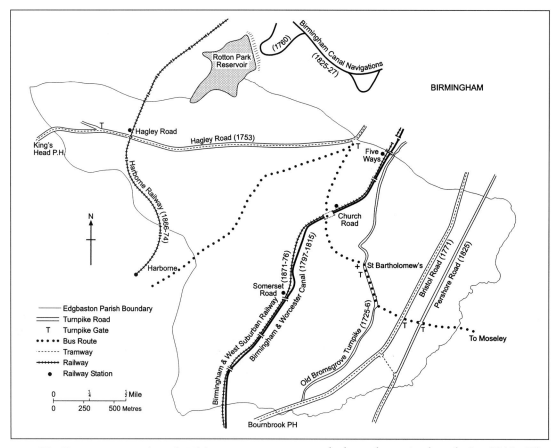

95 Transport routes through Edgbaston.

96 The south entrance to the Church Road canal tunnel.

opened throughout its length in 1815. The section through Edgbaston, which was opened in 1797, is both spectacular and picturesque. It crosses the valley of the Bourn Brook on a massive embankment, before entering a shallow cutting through the sandstone ridge on the north side of the park and a short tunnel under Church Road. The lengths of the canal on embankments required careful maintenance, of course, and in May 1872 the canal bank burst in Edgbaston, causing serious flooding in Gough, Pakenham and Charlotte Roads. Today the canal provides a semi-rural green route into the heart of the city centre from Selly Oak and the University of Birmingham.

One of the continuing problems for Birmingham's canal companies was to ensure a sufficient supply of water to operate the flights of locks which took boats down to the surrounding river valleys. Each time a boat

97 The flood caused by the bursting of the canal bank in 1872.

98 Sailing on Rotton Park reservoir, 1949.

99 Mainline express train approaching Church Road tunnel on the Birmingham & West Suburban line. The house is 'Southfield', home of Jesse Collings, MP in the late 19th century.

passes through a flight of locks, whether it is going up or down, it transfers a lock-full of water from the top of the system to the bottom. Since there were hundreds of boats using the canals each week this meant that a lot of water was required and a plateau-top location like Birmingham's is not an easy place to find such large quantities of water. It was for this reason that the end of the Birmingham and Worcester Canal, in the Gas Street Basin, was marked by a stone bar. In this way water was not transferred from the Worcester Canal into the Birmingham Canal Company's canals or vice versa; unfortunately, this also meant that goods had to be unloaded from one boat into another across the bar.

The Birmingham Canal Company resolved their water supply problem in 1825-7 when Thomas Telford was modernising the canal to Smethwick and Wolverhampton by using the techniques that were soon to be utilised in constructing railways. The new broad, arrow-straight, mainline canal, with its double towpath, ran in cuttings and across embankments bisecting the loops of its contour-based predecessor of the 1760s. The water supply was ensured by constructing a large reservoir in Rotton Park, on the north side of Edgbaston, where there was already a marshy pool. Though it was fed naturally by only a tiny stream, Telford constructed piped aqueducts from the north to provide additional supplies of water for the reservoir with its capacity of 300 million gallons. There was also a pumping engine to raise any surplus water in the canal up into the reservoir. Its massive brick-faced earth dam remains an impressive feature of the Edgbaston landscape, whilst the tree-planted perimeter of the 60-acre pool provides for walkers and wildlife; however, technically only the southern quarter of the reservoir is in the historic parish.

Only 20 years after its construction the reservoir was already being regarded as an important amenity. A directory of 1849 describes it as a place which 'in picturesque beauty can scarcely be surpassed by a natural lake. On Sundays it is liberally thrown open to the public and, indeed, is at all times accessible to respectable persons by application to the Lodge'. By the late 19th century it was an important recreational resource for the increasingly built-up area around. In 1873 the famous acrobat and tightrope walker, Blondin, showed off his agility and skill to large crowds; more tragically, four boys were drowned in the summer of 1877. The YMCA held a regatta there each year and the Midland Sailing Club built their headquarters at the north end of the dam in 1910. A lido for swimming was opened in the 1930s, on the south side of the reservoir, and a roller-skating rink also on the south side, whilst a cafeteria had been added to the facilities by the main entrance by then. After the Second World War, the roller-skating rink was upgraded to become the Tower Ballroom, whilst Butlins constructed a mini-funfair near the main entrance. The pool continued to be heavily used for angling and water sports, including sailing and windsurfing, throughout the 20th century.

Railways
Neither the Calthorpe family nor the well-to-do residents of Edgbaston were ever likely to show any favour to the presence of the noise and smoke of the railway locomotive. Though present-day rail travellers to and from the southwest of England are familiar with a route that closely follows the Birmingham and Worcester Canal from Bournville to Birmingham's New Street station, this was not the original main line to Gloucester and Bristol; that went through Moseley and Kings Heath. The line beside the canal, through Edgbaston, was incorporated as the Birmingham West Suburban Railway in 1871, and was opened and taken over by the Midland Railway in 1876. To begin with it was a single track from Kings Norton, with no

connection to New Street. It had stations at Bournville, Selly Oak, Somerset Road and Church Road. The Midland Railway saw its potential and gained an Act in 1881 to double the tracks, close the Granville Street terminus, and connect the line to New Street, providing a new station at Five Ways. The rebuilding was enormously costly because of tunnelling and cuttings into the city centre. It became the main line to Gloucester and Bristol in 1885 and eventually the three Edgbaston stations were closed, but in the later 20th century the needs of commuters were again attended to and the new Cross-City service, developed in 1978, saw the opening of new stations at Five Ways and University.

Edgbaston's first railway had been promoted in 1866 when the Harborne Railway Act was passed in Parliament, but the line was not opened until 1874. There was significant opposition to the plan by both the Calthorpe and Gillott estates, which insisted on substantial compensation and 'green' embankments, not viaducts, for the line. This tiny railway was an independent company but was operated by the London and North Western Railway (LNWR). The single-track line left the Wolverhampton main line at Monument Lane and had stations at Icknield Port Road, Rotton Park Road and Hagley Road, before terminating on the north side of Harborne. The journey on the somewhat optimistically named 'Harborne Express' from New Street took about 20 minutes on an hourly schedule and the trains were operated by little 2-4-2 tank engines. Passenger services lasted only until 1934, but the line remained open for goods services until the closures following the Beeching Report in 1963. Part of the route through Edgbaston was converted into a walkway and cycle route by the city council.

Buses and Trams
Municipal tramways were authorised by the Birmingham Corporation Act of 1903, but it was not until 1907 that new electric trams were seen on the streets of Edgbaston. Since trams

100   Bristol Road trams near Sir Harry's Road, *c*.1910.

101   The Bristol Road was made a dual carriageway with trams in the central reservation in 1924. This view of the crossing at Eastern Road was taken in 1937.

102 The Moseley bus beginning its climb up Edgbaston Park Road, 1925.

were perceived of as a working-class form of transport, the residents of Edgbaston did not welcome the development. There was considerable opposition to the prospect of trams along the Hagley Road with its prestigious mansions, and both Lord Calthorpe and Neville Chamberlain, the local MP, were amongst those to voice opposition, claiming they would detract from the solitude and quiet of Edgbaston, and reduce property values. However, in 1912 another Act of Parliament provided the authority for Birmingham Corporation to build a tramway along Holloway Head to Five Ways and then along the Hagley Road to the *Kings Head* public house. A year later the trams were running and continued to do so until 1930, when the route was one of the first to be converted to

motor buses. In 1914 there was an interesting three-month experiment with a 'first-class' service but custom was insufficient.

Opposition to trams was much less on the Bristol Road, partly because there were fewer houses and their occupants less prestigious, partly because the road was nearer the edge of the parish, and partly because there was a longer tradition of tramways there. The original horse-buses had been superseded by a horse-drawn tramway in 1873 which terminated at the *Bournbrook Hotel*. Horses continued to be used until 1890, when this route was the first to be converted to battery-operated 48-seater electric trams. Conversion to overhead mains electricity took place in 1901 when the City of Birmingham Tramway Co. extended the line to Selly Oak using 15 cars on the route. Soon after, in 1904, the tramway was extended to Cotteridge by building lines down Pebble Mill Road and along the Pershore Road. Pebble Mill Road was used as a model for Birmingham's arterial road construction in 1919, with the dual carriageway planted with avenues of trees and the central reservation reserved for the tram tracks. It was so successful that in 1924 the Bristol Road route was rebuilt in the central reservation. The route was one of the last to be closed, in 1952, and was used to store tramcars before they were sent for scrap.

Midland Red

Given the antipathy of Edgbaston's principal residents to all forms of public transport, it is surprising to find that Edgbaston was the headquarters of Britain's largest bus company in the inter-war period. In 1904 the Birmingham & Midland Motor Omnibus Co. Ltd (the proper name of 'Midland Red' until 1974) had begun operating motor buses along the Harborne and Hagley Roads. These early buses regularly broke

down and from 1907 to 1912 the company reverted to horse-buses. In 1912 new petrol-electric Tilling-Stevens vehicles were introduced and proved much more reliable, but when the Hagley Road tram service opened the bus service had to close. The following year Midland Red and the corporation agreed not to compete with one another: corporation trams would develop routes within the city and Midland Red would develop routes from the city centre to communities beyond the city boundary. Midland Red vehicles were maintained in a depot in Bearwood until the end of the First World War but the company then acquired workshops from the Daimler Co. in Carlyle Road, Edgbaston, who had been using them to produce aircraft parts. Between 1920 and 1924 all the company's repair, assembly and construction work was transferred to Carlyle Road. In 1954 the 50th anniversary of the company was marked by the opening of the new purpose-built Central Works, which was widely acclaimed in the technical press for its 'state-of-the-art' layout and facilities.

Ten

Higher Education:
the University of Birmingham

If there is one institution that dominates the history of 20th-century Edgbaston it must be the University of Birmingham, whose extensive campus stretches from the Bourn Brook, in the south, half-way across the parish to Church Road in the north. The university began, however, not in Edgbaston, but in the city centre, in Edmund Street on the north side of what is now Chamberlain Square. This was the site of Sir Josiah Mason's Science College. Mason was one of Birmingham's richest industrialists. He made his initial fortune by developing a cheap process for making steel pen nibs. By 1875 his works were producing more than 4½ million a week! He invested some of his profits in George Elkington's process of electro-plating and made another fortune. He was knighted in 1872 for his charitable work in setting up Birmingham's largest orphanage. The final project of his long life was to found a higher education college to teach science and mathematics. Similar schemes were being proposed in other cities in the 1860s and '70s as the provincial demand for scientific, rather than classical, higher education began to escalate. However, most of these were co-operative ventures by the city élites rather than the venture of one person.

Mason laid the foundation stone on his 80th birthday, 23 February 1875, and the college was opened amidst great civic celebration on 1 October 1880. The building provided for the teaching of biology, chemistry,

mathematics and physics initially, but the range of subjects expanded quickly over the next decade and the medical school from Queen's College was incorporated into Mason College in 1892. Two years later the first steps were taken towards the conversion of the college to a university. To begin with, there was no thought of an independent institution; rather, a federal 'university of the Midlands' was the vision, similar to the Victoria University federation in northern industrial cities. The change in vision came in 1896 when the opinion of

103   Professor J.H. Poynting DSc., FRS, JP: Poynting was the foundation professor of physics and one of the five original professors of Mason College.

Joseph Chamberlain, former mayor and now at the heart of government, was sought. He was vehemently against joining the Victoria University. The following year, inspired by a visit to Glasgow University, he determined there should be a University of Birmingham, unencumbered by federation with other midland colleges. He knew this would require a large sum of money for endowment and buildings and so took charge of the necessary appeal. The college was incorporated in 1898 and the appeal was launched in July of that year. Chamberlain was well aware of the need for a small number of large donors and persuaded the Canadian railway magnate, Lord Strathcona, and the American steel magnate, Andrew Carnegie, to provide £50,000 each. Carnegie also insisted that a group should tour American universities. This changed the vision once more, since the group returned with a report extolling the virtues of the spacious science campuses they had seen.

104 Professor Sir Oliver Lodge: Lodge was the university's first principal and was knighted in 1902.

'The Birmingham University Act 1900' received royal assent on 25 May. The governors met for the first time six days later, and the first principal, Professor Oliver Lodge, was appointed. The new university set a new pattern for higher education of academic self-government balanced by support from, and accountability to, the local community—the civic university. In July came a gift that was to allow Birmingham to become another first, the first campus university in Britain. In that month Lord Calthorpe wrote offering a site of 25 acres in Edgbaston for the science departments. This allowed the new building that was so necessary to take place but at the cost of a split site for the university; it was to be sixty years before arts and science were reunited.

University Buildings

The site was a rectangle on the plateau top above the Bourn Brook, with a field used as a rifle range below. A new access road, University Road, was provided to the north, and Calthorpe insisted that the entrance to the university be on this northern side. The architects appointed (by Chamberlain) to design the university buildings were the London firm of Aston Webb and Ingress Bell, one of the foremost practices of the day. Local people were infuriated, but Chamberlain was determined that people were going to notice 'his' university. They decided to use the slope to exaggerate the height of the buildings and use the promontory to give a semi-circular form to the whole; the overall impression which they wanted to create was that of an Italian city on a hill. In detail they conceived of a half-wheel design, with an east-west block of buildings facing University Road including an impressive central entrance, and then a series of 'T'-shaped buildings, with domes atop their inner ends, arranged like the spokes of a wheel to the south. The final design was for seven spokes, the central one being a grand ceremonial hall with a cupola tower at the north end which was later omitted. Work began in September 1901, and by 1905 three of the radial

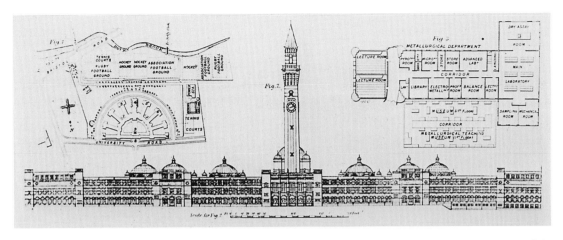

105 Aston Webb and Ingress Bell, plan of University: the overall plan, a plan of one wing and the façade of the north front as conceived by the architects.

106 The University under construction, *c*.1902: this photograph, by Sir Benjamin Stone, shows the Great Hall and the three wings that were first constructed.

blocks, and the terminal blocks of the north front, were ready for occupation. Work then moved to the Great Hall, which was completed in 1909 together with the entrance block with the library above, all in time for the visit of Edward VII on 7 July (Chamberlain's 73rd birthday) to open the new university buildings. There was also a power station for the university to make its own electricity and gas, which could also be used for teaching purposes, and a 'mine' with a mile of underground galleries in brick and concrete for the department of mining.

All this was expensive and it was known from the start that the building would have to be phased. The initial plan was for four spoke

107 Rt Hon. Joseph Chamberlain as Chancellor: it was thanks to the drive and enthusiasm of Chamberlain that the University was founded and he became its first Chancellor, 1900-14.

108 The University from the south gate, *c*.1909.

buildings and the frontage blocks, but as the Great Hall was increased in size and cost, becoming considerably larger than the Town Hall, one of the spokes had to be sacrificed. The buildings were also decorated in the most splendid manner. The Great Hall, in particular, was clearly meant to be a prestigious building announcing to the world that Birmingham had a first-class university.

The structure which dominates the university, and Edgbaston, however, is not the Great Hall but the clock tower. At 325 feet high it is still the second tallest building in Birmingham and can be seen from miles around. A tower had been a feature of the design from the beginning but its form and location changed frequently. Chamberlain, however, was determined to have a clock tower and in 1905 was able to report an anonymous donation (from Sir Charles Holcroft) of £50,000 for a tower. Aston Webb revised his plans and a free-standing tower in the middle of the semi-circular court was decided upon, the design being based on the Torre di Mangia in Sienna. Work began in 1906 with a massive concrete base for the foundation and was nearly complete in time for the king's visit in 1909. The tower is of red Accrington brick with Darley Dale stone dressings and was built from the inside, without scaffolding. Pointing of the exterior brickwork was carried out only in 1914, by workmen suspended from the top in cages, when it was realised that the sloping sides of the tower allowed rainwater to penetrate the brickwork. There is a lift up to the gigantic clock and bells. The clock faces are just over 17 feet in diameter and have white reflective bricks behind the luminescent glass to improve its readability from distance. The clock was a gift from the main building contractors, Thomas Rowbottom. The largest of the four bells is more than six tons in weight. 'Old Joe', as the clock tower became affectionately known to generations of students, is a worthy memorial to the effective founder and first chancellor of the University of Birmingham.

Military Hospital

The scientists at the university enjoyed their new accommodation for only nine years. With the outbreak of the First World War the buildings were requisitioned for the First Southern General Hospital. This military hospital had 520 beds and was ready for action within seven days! The women's hall of residence, University House, was also requisitioned as a nurses' home, and the university had to return to the city centre. The university medical faculty constituted a large part of the staff of the hospital. As the first casualties were brought in, the hospital was extended to take 800 patients by the end of 1914, and 1,000 a year later. By the Armistice there were 3,293 beds, some of them in marquees in the courtyard, and more than 64,000 patients had passed through the hospital. Many staff and students were killed at the front and the university war memorial records 175 names, one of whom, John Marshall, was awarded the Victoria Cross.

Chemistry, Physics and Art

The inter-war years were dominated by the pressing needs of rebuilding staff resources, dealing with recurrent financial difficulties, and reorganising academic departments and governance. New buildings for biology, oil (later chemical) engineering (which included a full-scale oil-drilling rig!) and chemistry were built at Edgbaston, and it was in the latter department that Professor W.N. Howarth was responsible for synthesising the first artificial vitamin C, an achievement recognised by the award of the Nobel Prize for Chemistry in 1937. The overall size of the campus had already increased with the gift of the rifle range alongside the Bourn Brook for playing fields, but in 1927 the campus was doubled in size when the Calthorpes gave the university 41 acres of land between University Road and Pritchatts Road. The first plan was to build another semi-circle of radial blocks to mirror the earlier buildings, but the Calthorpes specified a new north entrance on Pritchatts Road and a processional

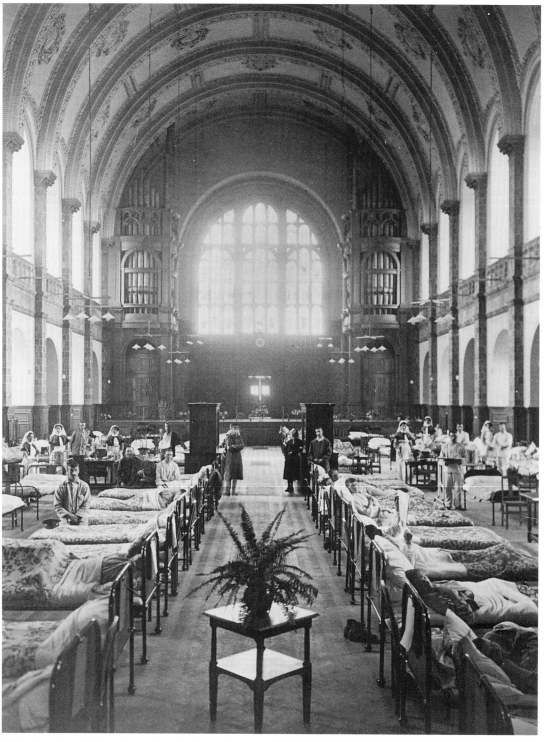

109 The Great Hall as hospital ward: during the First World War the university was requisitioned as the First Southern General Hospital.

110 The University buildings from the south: this fine drawing from the playing fields to the south is by Henry Rushbury RA.

avenue. The lodges, semi-circular concourse, and wrought-iron entrance gates were designed by a local architect, William Haywood. They led to a double avenue of Lombardy poplars and limes, 330 yards long and 50 feet wide, leading to the Harding Library entrance gates on University Road.

The other major building of the inter-war years, standing prominently at the Edgbaston Park Road end of the campus, was the Barber Institute of Fine Arts, now regarded as one of Britain's finest small art galleries. Sir Henry Barber was a Birmingham solicitor turned property developer. He endowed the professorship of law in 1923, and after his death Lady Barber decided to establish a trust which was to build an institute of fine arts and purchase paintings of the highest quality for it. She died in 1933 and the trustees appointed Robert Atkinson to design the institute. It is an Art Deco building of high quality, unmistakeably of its time inside and out, and recently cleaned and restored by the trustees. It was formally opened by Queen Elizabeth in 1939. The first

director, Thomas Bodkin, besides acquiring paintings, also purchased the magnificent equestrian statue of George I which stands in front of the institute. It was made by the Flemish sculptor Jan Van Nost for Dublin Corporation in 1722, and was in imminent danger of destruction from Irish republicans in 1930s' Dublin.

The university's principal contribution to the Second World War came from the physics department, where two teams of researchers discovered, first, how to control short-wave radio waves by a cavity magnetron, which led rapidly to the development of a practicable radar system, an absolutely vital ingredient in the winning of the war and, secondly, the work which led to the development of the first atomic bomb. This came from the work of Professor of Physics, Mark Oliphant, and the German applied mathematicians, Rudolf Peierls and Otto Frisch. The initial discoveries were made in Birmingham but the team was then transferred to Liverpool, and soon afterwards, in 1943, to the USA, where the Manhattan Project was set up.

111 The University from the north, *c.*1925: the rural situation of the University in the inter-war period still surprises.

112 Student celebrations at opening of North Gates, 1930: the grand avenue of Lombardy poplars and the new north gates were celebrated by a procession of student motor-bikes!

113   The Barber Institute of Fine Arts and the statue of George I.

Extending the Campus

In 1944, the university appointed the architect Verner Rees to develop plans for the north side of the campus in terms of a new library, a building for arts, commerce and law, and a new refectory. These would allow the evacuation of the city centre buildings in Edmund Street and the final integration of the university on a single site. Difficulties with finance, building permits and planning meant that it was to be the late 1950s before these plans came to fruition. The major debate was whether the avenue should be retained, with the new buildings placed symmetrically on each side, or whether it could be removed to allow a new square to be created. The second scheme was eventually to find favour. The new library was begun in 1956 and opened officially by Queen Elizabeth, the Queen Mother in 1960, and the arts building followed in the same year, both designed by Verner Rees.

The university's other priority was for student residences. University House, for women students, had been built in 1904 and a male hostel had been opened as Chancellor's Hall in 1921 in Augustus Road. Immediately after the war the university began to acquire houses and land along Edgbaston Park Road. 'Winterbourne' came by bequest in 1944 and became an annexe of University House; land in 'the Vale' in 1947; the rest of 'the Vale', 'Wyddrington', and 'Maple Bank', in Church Road were purchased from the Calthorpe estate in 1955; 'Westmere' became the staff club through the 1950s and '60s; and 'Meadowcroft' was purchased in 1953 for the Vice-Chancellor's residence. The initial ideas for new halls on the Vale site were for a series of high-rise towers, but in 1957 the university appointed new estate architects, Sir Hugh Casson and Neville Conder, whose first task was to provide a plan for the 45 acres of land now available for development. They provided two plans: the first was for a series of replacement large houses set in the existing gardens; the other for a number of modern buildings in a new open landscape reminiscent of the parks of the 18th century. It was the latter that was to be brought to fruition in what is widely regarded as one of the finest halls complexes of any British university.

The landscape was designed by Mary Mitchell and involved the excavation of a new lake, the considerable remodelling of the contours of the site, but also the retention of many mature trees from the earlier villa gardens. The open fringe of the site, especially along Edgbaston Park Road, provides an important amenity and prospect for local residents. Finance came from an appeal which raised nearly £1½ million in the latter half of 1960.

Architects Casson and Conder were meanwhile having rather less success with their plans for the expansion of the main campus. They seem to have been determined to do everything they could to break the coherence of the Aston and Bell and the Rees plans, of semi-circle and large square respectively. There were unexecuted plans for building on much of the Bournbrook playing fields, for tunnelling under the Great Hall, and for building in the middle of University Square! None of this came to fruition. However, it is thanks to them that the

114 University House hall of residence: University House was designed by W.T. Buckland in 1904-8 as the first hall of residence for women.

115 Student room in University House: this homely view shows a student's room in the 1920s.

116 Chancellor's Hall: the University purchased 'The Dales' in Augustus Road in 1921, the former home of George Dixon MP, as the nucleus of the first hall for men.

117 Architect's sketch of High Hall, the Vale: the architects provided the university with a series of polished drawings to show what the new halls of residence would look like.

118   The Vale landscape with Wyddrington and High Halls.

119   Muirhead Tower completed in 1967 by Arup Associates.

'gaps' in the Aston Webb buildings of the semi-circle still remain and that the outer fringes of the campus consist of unrelated 'pavilion' buildings. More positively, University Road was closed to pedestrianise University Square, and a ring road was provided for traffic circulation. The most controversial of the new buildings was Muirhead Tower, which provides a vertical accent in the north-east corner of University Square and was for the social science departments. It is an uncompromising 'Brutalist' concrete building, completed in 1967 to the design of Philip Dowson of Arup Associates. Whilst it gained a Civic Trust commendation for its design, its inadequate lifts, poorly fixed windows and 'wind-tunnel' podium have made it the most disliked building on the campus for generations of students and staff, as well as the university estate office! Recently, the west gate of the university has been marked by a sculpture, a massive work called 'Faraday', the gift of the artist Sir Eduardo Paolozzi.

Other Higher Education Institutions

The Queen's College was founded in 1828 by William Sands Cox FRS (1801-75), a local surgeon, as the Birmingham School of Medicine and Surgery. A teaching hospital was added in 1843 which, under royal patronage, was called the Queen's Hospital in Birmingham, so the medical school became Queen's College. Its mission was expanded to teach architecture, the arts, civil engineering, the law and theology. Unfortunately, competition from the General Hospital and Sands Cox's unwillingness to delegate meant that the affairs of the college became chaotic and bankruptcy threatened. The affairs of the college and the hospital were separated in 1867 and the curriculum was concentrated on the arts, medicine and theology. Medical and dental training in the city was combined and eventually moved to Mason College.

By 1872 arts teaching had been dropped, an attempt to start a course in trade and

120 Paolozzi's statue 'Faraday', given to the University of Birmingham for its centenary in 2000.

121 William Sands Cox FRS.

commerce was not a success, and even theology was at a low ebb. Queen's College occupied buildings in Paradise Street, opposite the Town Hall, the attractive façade of which still survives. The support of the Anglican Church meant that theology teaching did continue and eventually, in 1936, its remaining activities were transferred to the former residence of the first Bishop of Birmingham in Somerset Road, Edgbaston. The neo-Gothic extravagance of this house led some to call it 'the ugliest house in Christendom'! It had been gifted to Queen's College some time before and was already being used for a hall of residence and for some teaching activities. In the 1960s it became an ecumenical theological college (Anglican-Methodist). The chapel dates from 1845 and has a stained glass window by Brook Smith.

Surprisingly, Edgbaston is host to at least a part of one of Birmingham's other two universities. The University of Central England occupies a substantial campus on Westbourne Road which is the home of the education, and health and community care faculties of the university, together with halls of residence. The site began as the City of Birmingham Teachers' Training College, set up immediately after the Second World War to combat the severe shortage of teachers in the city. In 1957 it moved into the purpose-built accommodation in Westbourne Road designed by Shepphard Fidler. The training college became one of the constituent institutions that went to make Birmingham Polytechnic and hence became part of UCE when it was founded because of the government policy of upgrading polytechnics to university status in 1990. Ravensbury House, on the opposite side of Westbourne Road, provides specialist facilities for non-medical health-care studies.

Eleven

Hospitals and Medical Facilities

Edgbaston became the home of most of Birmingham's most eminent doctors in the 19th century but it was not until the mid-20th century that it became the most important medical centre in Birmingham with the opening of the Queen Elizabeth Hospital and the University Medical School in 1938-9. Planning for this second major 'campus' in Edgbaston had begun in 1925, when it was agreed that the university medical school should transfer from Edmund Street to Edgbaston. It was clear that new hospital facilities were needed in Birmingham and that, logically, the best place for teaching hospitals was beside the medical school. The idea of the 'Hospital's Centre Scheme' was that over a period of time a constellation of new hospitals should be built on an extensive medical campus. The other stimulus was the difficulty of extending the General and Queen's hospitals on their city centre sites. Such a scheme inevitably needed both land and money and an appeal was launched to finance the plan in April 1930. By June £478,000 had been promised and by the end of the year this had increased to £584,000. As with any appeal, a number of major donors had been determined from the beginning. These included Sir Harry Vincent, the treasurer, who gave £250,000; Lord Nuffield, who gave £198,000 for the nurses' home; Messrs Cadbury Bros Ltd, whose £100,000 secured the land; and £20,000 from the city council which paid for the new access roads and their tree-lined verges, notably Vincent Drive, the extension

to University Road, and the large roundabout in front of the medical school. These roads were scheduled as 'private', under the control of the university and hospital, so as to control through traffic. This was a wise precaution because, a few years previously, the Ministry of Transport had proposed a major traffic arterial across the site as part of a new road from Coventry to Wolverhampton, bypassing the city centre. The university had declared that it would have to move if such a scheme were to be implemented.

The planning committee, with university vice-chancellor Grant Robertson in the chair, consisted of equal representation from the university, the General Hospital and Queen's Hospital, and it was agreed that the first buildings should be the medical school, an acute general hospital, and its nurses' home. The 100-acre site had been purchased in 1926 by Cadbury's and gifted to the city council. Only the northern half was suitable for building and the area beside the Bourn Brook was expressly reserved for allotments. The transfer deed also specified that buildings with chimneys had to be at the southern end of the site to preserve residential amenities in Edgbaston, and that hospitals for mental illness and infectious diseases were prohibited. Sites were allotted not only for the initial buildings, but for all the other specialist hospitals proposed, including dental, maternity and ear and throat hospitals. An architectural competition was held for the design of the medical school and general hospital and

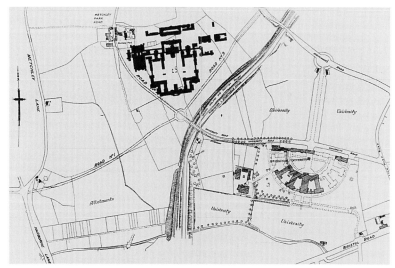

122 Plan of proposed roads and hospital: this plan shows how the university and medical campuses are divided by canal and railway. The new roads were private initially.

123 Drawing of Medical School and QE Hospital: this fine drawing shows the relationship of the Medical School (left) and the Queen Elizabeth Hospital (right).

attracted a large number of entries. Plans and drawings were displayed in the city art gallery for judging, and to encourage people to give to the appeal. The winners were Messrs Lanchester and Lodge. The planning committee were anxious to have a unified architectural scheme for the campus and each hospital had agreed to consult on design and building materials to 'avoid the loss of dignity of design which has so often disfigured our city in the past'. Unfortunately, such was the delay in providing for even the first of these additional hospitals, the maternity, that architectural styles had changed dramatically and the hospitals'

campus has deteriorated into the architectural mess that the planning committee had been so anxious to avoid.

Lanchester and Lodge provided a classic Art Deco design that gets its power and attraction from the massing of forms and the unity of the 'golden yellow-brown' bricks that were used, some four million in total! The medical school is a long three/four-storey building with an elegant entrance emphasised by modest use of Portland stone and a sculptural plaque above. The Queen Elizabeth Hospital, as the acute general was to be called, is a six-storey building, with basement levels below; all the wards are designed to face south to maximise sunshine, and as many of the interior dividing walls as possible were designed to be non-load-bearing. The original plan had been for a 750-bed hospital but, as local and national planning authorities delayed the start of building to 1933, inflation meant that only 540 beds could be provided. The 180-bed west wing, together with out-patients and casualty departments, was left until more money could be raised. As any visitor to the QE knows today, these parts of the building were never to be completed.

The medical school was ready for occupation in 1937 and the hospital at the very end of 1938, after five years of construction work and at a cost of over £1 million, almost all of which was met by voluntary donations. During the Second World War the QE took in twice the number of patients for which it was designed, as it received casualties not only from the air raids on Birmingham, but those injured in the evacuation from Dunkirk, in the North African campaign, and in the D-Day landings. The hospital had its own coal-fired heating plant and its own well for water supply, the central tower of the hospital building

124 *Above right.* The Medical School entrance front.

125 *Right.* Medical School and QE Hospital, *c*.1950: the un-finished western wing and casualty department (where the huts are located) was never to be completed.

126 The high-tech cancer research centre is one of the most recent buildings on the medical campus.

containing water storage tanks for 120,000 gallons. The nurses' home, Nuffield House, was on the northern side of the hospital and its eight floors provided rooms for 300 nurses and the nurses' training school. Its huge 'recreation hall' can seat a thousand people when dividing screens are drawn back.

Only two of the other hospitals that were intended for the site were eventually constructed after the war. The first was the Maternity Hospital in the early 1960s, which was refurbished in the early 1990s when it took over the functions of the Women's Hospital as well. The second was the Psychiatric Hospital. Both the Queen Elizabeth Hospital and the Medical School have been extended and there are now plans for a new general hospital to combine the functions of both the Queen Elizabeth and Selly Oak on a single site.

Specialist and Private Hospitals

Birmingham's Children's Hospital had relocated to the old lying-in hospital in Broad Street in 1869, but well before the end of the century it was realised that the building was too small for the very large number of patients being seen. In 1907 the governors resolved to build a completely new hospital on a site at Five Ways in Ladywood Road. Money came from the wave of patriotic emotion which the death of Edward VII evoked, and was channelled into a memorial fund by the *Birmingham Daily Mail*,

which raised £30,000. Building was delayed by the outbreak of war and it was late in 1917 before the first patients were moved in. Its nurses' home was added in 1929. The hospital was closed at the end of the century on its removal to the refurbished General Hospital on another wave of patriotic emotion, becoming the Diana, Princess of Wales Children's Hospital. The Five Ways site is being redeveloped as a shopping and entertainments complex.

The Skin Hospital had been in John Bright Street in its own building since 1888 but a need for increased in-patient treatment saw its removal to George Road, Edgbaston in 1933. No. 35, a small nursing home, was purchased and a new ward block laid out in the grounds. It celebrated its centenary in 1981. The Midland Nerve Hospital has a similar history, relocating in the later 19th century to 'The Firs' on the corner of Ryland and Charlotte Roads, where new buildings were added in the garden. The hospital site was purchased by the University of Birmingham in the 1990s and student flats called 'The Beeches' were built there. Edgbaston also became home to three private health facilities as private health care expanded from the 1970s onwards. The Priory Hospital in Priory Road and the Nuffield Hospital in Somerset Road provide a wide range of private treatments whilst the Edgbaston Health Clinic specialises in sports-related injuries.

Twelve

Education I:
King Edward's Schools

Origins

Like many Edgbaston institutions, for most of its long history King Edward's School (KES) was located in the city centre, and it was only in the middle of the 20th century that it moved out to the suburban fields of Edgbaston. It was founded on 2 January 1552 as a consequence of the suppression of the religious guilds by King Edward VI in 1547. The year 2002 therefore marks its 450th anniversary. One of the guilds suppressed was the Holy Cross Guild in Birmingham. The Act of Suppression had allowed that any school which had been supported by a guild could retain guild lands with rents up to £20 per annum to allow the school to continue to provide an education to local children. Consequently there are a large number of King Edward VI schools in England. However, Birmingham's is different because the guild of the Holy Cross did not support a school. Rather, the members of the guild petitioned the king to be allowed to found a new school supported by former guild rents to the value of £20. The reason they were successful was probably that they had the support of the Earl of Northumberland, at that time the most important statesman in the country, and lord of the manor of Birmingham. It was the quick opportunism and boldness of the leading citizens of the town that enabled them to establish the new free grammar school, which was established in the old guild building on the south side of New Street. The school was

replaced twice on this site, first in 1731-4 and then almost exactly a century later in 1838.

By the last quarter of the 19th century attitudes towards education were changing rapidly, especially in the fast growing industrial towns such as Birmingham. In these places the close-knit industrial élite, who had made their fortunes from science and industry, had moved on in later life to take on civic responsibility and lead social reform, prompted often by strongly held religious views. Such men were aware of the importance of a scientifically and mathematically educated group who could be trained to manage the enormous variety of new enterprises being developed in their cities; and they wanted their daughters to become useful members of society, too, especially since one in five women were destined never to marry because of the national gender imbalance in this period. Consequently, there was a desire for a wider-based education system for all children, a recognition of the need for more 'middle schools' to educate children between the ages of 13 and 16, and the desire for a post-16 'high school' for girls to match the provision of KES for boys. To this end, in 1881 the school's governing body, the King Edward's Foundation, decided to establish a new high school for girls and five other grammar schools in the suburbs of the town, one at Aston and one at Five Ways for boys, one at Handsworth for girls, and two at Camp Hill, one for boys and one for girls. The King

127   Edgbaston Proprietary School, Hagley Road, *c.*1860.

Edward's High School for Girls (KEHS), opened in 1883 with an intake of 150 girls selected by entrance examination, was located in part of the boys' New Street building. It expanded rapidly and moved first to Congreve Street and then, in 1893, to a new building next to the boys school with accommodation for 300 girls. Miss Creak, the first headmistress, had been educated at Cambridge in science and was determined that the new school should have the best science laboratories of any girls school in England. Consequently, the quality of its scientific education rapidly gained a national reputation.

Five Ways
King Edward's School, Five Ways, occupied an earlier school building on the north side of the Hagley Road, the Birmingham and Edgbaston Proprietary School, built in neo-Tudor style. This was purchased by the King

Edward's Foundation in 1882. The new school was intended for 350 boys and so it was adapted and enlarged, to designs by J.A. Chatwin, who did so much work in Edgbaston, to include six extra classrooms and a library. Further extensions were made in 1909-10 for science laboratories, an art room and a gymnasium. The school building was demolished as part of the Five Ways traffic island and underpass improvements and the school was relocated to a spacious site in Bartley Green in 1958.

To Edgbaston
By the 1920s the financial strains of supporting seven independent schools with some 2,700 pupils, particularly in the light of the economic situation nationally, had become too much for the Foundation, which had an income of only some £100,000, and so financial support had to be sought from the city council. After the Second World War a more satisfactory and

longer-term solution was found by converting the schools into direct grant grammar schools under the 1944 Education Act, though the schools were allowed to maintain their separate entrance examination to supplement the 11-plus results. However, in 1932 the financial crisis was immediate, and the Foundation reluctantly decided that the city centre schools would have to be given up in order to finance new buildings and facilities. They therefore purchased 30 acres of land in Edgbaston from the Calthorpe estate and the following year appointed Holland W. Hobbiss FRIBA, an old Edwardian, as architect for the new schools.

The new buildings were to be financed from the sale of the old, and temporary buildings were therefore required on the new site.

KES had occupied its building in New Street for almost exactly a century; KEHS had occupied their building for only forty years but, at the end of 1935, the two schools vacated the much-loved premises and, to the considerable regret of many former pupils and Birmingham citizens, the schools were demolished. The new schools were located adjacent to one another on an extensive, sloping site, close to the university, in the angle of Edgbaston Park Road and Bristol Road. However, their construction had yet to

128   The Sturge memorial and King Edward's Five Ways, *c.*1900.

129 A corridor from the New Street school was dismantled and re-erected on the new site as the school chapel.

130 The aftermath of the fire at the temporary school, 1936.

131 The rebuilt temporary schools, now with fire escapes from each classroom.

be started. In January 1936, therefore, they moved into temporary wooden buildings on the Bristol Road frontage of the new property designed by Hobbiss. These were in the form of a double rectangle enclosing two garden courts for each school, with assembly halls separating the two courts. Administrative offices formed an entrance block between the two. The autumn was extremely wet, so the construction site was a sea of mud for much of the time. Whilst the building was going on staff began to store school treasures, such as paintings, honours boards, and library furniture in 'Park Vale', one of the two houses on the site.

On 14 January 1936 a fleet of buses bought boys and girls from town, and others came by bicycle. Excited pupils were met by a building whose whole exterior was painted a dull yellow, but the interiors were in a variety of pastel shades and Miss Barrie, the girls' head, thoughtfully provided a vase of anemones in each classroom of the girls' school on the opening day. In a similar spirit, Mr E.T. England, the headmaster of KES, planted masses of daffodils alongside the main paths to each school entrance for a blaze of spring colour. To begin with, lunches had to be provided in the university

refectory a few minutes walk away, since the dining rooms were unfinished, an early example of subsequent good relationships between the two educational institutions. Paradoxically, since one of the reasons for moving from New Street had been the poor fire prevention facilities in the old buildings, five months later, in the early morning of 6 May, the boys school was totally destroyed by fire to the extent that only the urinals were left standing above the ashes, whilst the girls school was so badly damaged it could not be used. The boys took their lessons in the Great Hall of the university for the summer term, whilst other classes were held in the brewing department! The girls evacuated to the Methodist Sunday School in Acocks Green where some lessons were held outside on the pavement in good weather!

The temporary schools were rebuilt in time for the autumn term but with brick walls dividing the classrooms, a fire exit from each room, fire doors in the corridors and a sprinkler system throughout. The first fire drill followed in October! All this might be seen as good practice for what was to follow since, in 1939, teachers of both schools were organising for evacuation if war were declared. The boys

132   KES Big School under construction. This was
the last building to be finished.

133   King Edward's Schools and Barber Institute,
c.1952: viewed from the clock tower, the newly
completed KES and KEHS await only the levelling of
their playing fields.

school found refuge at Repton School in Derbyshire, the girls at Pate's Grammar School in Cheltenham. In both cases the host school had lessons in the mornings, the visitors in the afternoons. A year later both schools decided to return to Birmingham, and they re-opened for the autumn term in September 1940 in their splendid (but unfinished) new buildings, which Hobbiss and his builders had continued to labour on, despite the shortage of materials. Lessons went on from 10 a.m. to 2.30 p.m. each day and there were bomb shelters under the buildings. Despite the heavy bombing of Birmingham, the schools escaped unscathed. The temporary buildings were then occupied by troops, including Americans in the later stages of the war, who, according to the school's historian, were a useful source of cigarettes for the young Kenneth Tynan, the theatre critic, then a pupil at KES.

Post-War Developments

KES was aided considerably in the period 1944-8 by headmaster Charles Morris. Morris had been a top civil servant in the Ministry of Supply and it was he who undertook the negotiations with the Ministry of Education for direct grant status. However, he had no time to attend to academic affairs before he left to become Vice Chancellor of Leeds University. In 1949 it came as an enormous shock to the staff of the school, and the Foundation, when an HMI report called the standards of teaching and examination results 'mediocre', with only music and art showing any signs of distinction. Consequently the teaching staff and their salaries were increased and the library substantially enlarged. The Chief Master who strides like a colossus across the second half of the 20th century now entered the scene. The Rev. Canon R.G. Lunt was an old Etonian and former chaplain to the Coldstream Guards and the Airborne Division, who had spent six years as head of Liverpool College before he was appointed to KES in 1952. He was Chief Master for 22 years and brought the school

back to its place in the highest rank of English schools in terms of academic standards.

As the curriculum expanded in the second half of the 20th century, new buildings were added, particularly to the boys school, including science laboratories (1959), a music school (1965), a language laboratory (1965), a drama studio (1985), an art and design centre (1990), and a computer and IT centre (1992). The girls school gained a new music room, and a sixth-form common room in 1960. Both schools continued to see sport and games as an important part of the curriculum. The new site had extensive playing fields on the Bristol Road frontage. The timber buildings (which had been occupied by the university since the Second

134 Canon Lunt, Chief Master 1952-74.

World War) were finally demolished in 1961, and this provided rugby and cricket pitches for the boys school. A new sports hall and squash courts were built on the Bristol Road frontage in 1971. An open-air swimming pool had been provided for the school in 1952 by Old Edwardians, as a war memorial gift, but this was replaced by an indoor pool in 1988. KEHS began using the field attached to Priorsfield House, then owned by Paul Cadbury, from 1948, and soon after permission to use his swimming pool and squash court was granted. Lack of adjacent playing fields was resolved in 1955 when the university sold the fields attached to 'Winterbourne' to the Foundation. They were levelled for tennis courts and hockey pitches, and more recently have been reconstructed with all-weather surfaces and floodlighting. A new swimming pool for the girls school was provided in 1964.

In 1976 the government began to phase out the direct grant scheme and the Foundation decided that the two schools should become independent, though making good use of the assisted places scheme provided. In 1987 Chief Master Martin Rogers of KES decided that economics meant that the school needed to expand and so it moved from four-form to five-form entry. Over the following seven years the number of boys therefore increased from 680 to 850. Many subsequently famous people have been pupils at the two schools, of course, but one of the best known, given our media-conscious age, is television presenter and wildlife enthusiast Bill Oddie. The school historian notes that he was a model pupil: prefect, member of the rugby first XV, and exhibitioner in English at Pembroke College, Cambridge; he remains legendary in Birmingham, though, for celebrating his leaving, with friends, by organising a series of mock road signs to direct traffic off Edgbaston Park Road, through the school grounds, and down to the Bristol Road, or so legend has it!

Thirteen

Education II:
Other Schools

Edgbaston is the 'education capital' of Birmingham and the history of all the schools located there in the past two centuries would more than fill a book of this size. What follows is therefore necessarily selective. There were no fewer than 12 secondary schools in Edgbaston in the 20th century, in addition to the schools of the King Edward Foundation. Two, Greenmore College and Park Grove, were private schools taking pupils more or less throughout the age range from junior to age eighteen. They stood almost opposite one another on the Bristol Road and amalgamated in the 1980s when the leases of the houses occupied by Greenmore College, on the corner of Priory Road, fell in and the site was redeveloped for modern housing. Park Grove occupied the attractive early 19th-century villa of that name in extensive grounds on the north side of Bristol Road. Nonetheless, the combined

school closed recently. Four more schools (St Philip's boys and St Paul's girls, Edgbaston C. of E. College, and Edgbaston High) reflect the denominational battles of the last quarter of the 19th century in educational provision and were all fee-paying to begin with. Finally, six (George Dixon, Lordswood boys and girls, Harborne Hill, Stanmore and Portland) reflect the increased provision by the state in the second half of the 20th century, following the 1944 Education Act and the post-war baby boom. However, we shall begin with a school which was far older than any of these institutions.

Hill Top and Hazelwood School

One of the earliest schools of which we know in Edgbaston was Hill Top. We know of it because it was founded by the father of Sir Rowland Hill. Rowland Hill was the son of a Kidderminster schoolmaster, and the family

135 Hazelwood School in Hagley Road: the building still survives.

103

moved to Edgbaston in 1803 where they established a school at the top end of Gough Street. Hill Top School was a great success over the next 16 years and both Rowland and his brother Frederic were pressed into service as assistant masters. In 1819 the school removed to a new building, designed by Rowland, on an extensive site in Hagley Road and was renamed 'Hazelwood'. It continued to expand and by 1822 had 150 boys aged 10-20 boarding there. Its reputation was certainly enhanced by Rowland's growing reputation as a scholar since he was a frequent lecturer at the Philosophical Institution in Birmingham. It ceases to be part of Edgbaston's history from 1827, when it was removed to London. Rowland stopped teaching in 1833 following a breakdown. He was knighted in 1860 for his work in reforming the Post Office, including the first use of postage stamps in 1840.

St Philip's and St Paul's schools

The two Roman Catholic grammar schools, St Philip's Grammar School for boys and St Paul's High School for girls, have their origins as adjuncts to the school attached to the Oratory, providing for more able pupils beyond age 13. They were part of the same aspirational desire for good quality secondary education beyond the age of 13 on the part of the new industrial middle classes which had led to the founding of the King Edward's Grammar Schools at much the same time. However, there was also a heartfelt argument between the proponents of non-sectarian education and those who believed that faith communities should be providing secondary education for their children. The boys school was established in 1887. There were only 30 boys initially, which was perhaps just as well as it began in an unfinished building of only two rooms in the grounds of St Philip's orphanage in Oliver Road. The Oratory fathers assisted with the teaching and the school developed slowly. By 1914 there were still only 132 boys on the roll. However, in 1922 the Oratory school was moved to Reading and the

more extensive buildings they occupied on the Hagley Road were converted for use by the grammar school. Evacuation at the beginning of the war was to Hereford Grammar School. The Oratory site was not extensive but post-1945 expansion demanded further new buildings which were added in 1957 and 1964. The houses on the Hagley Road frontage were condemned as unsafe and had to be demolished in 1968, making way for a new sixth-form centre. Pupil reminiscences suggest that St Philip's was a 'tough' school compared with most in Edgbaston; corporal punishment was frequent, bullying endemic, and it was no place for the sensitive.

In 1976 it was decided to concentrate resources by becoming a co-educational sixth-form college. The policy was successful and the college thrived in its local community, offering 30 different subjects at A-Level GCE. That community was changing, however, and by 1985 the school reflected its multi-ethnic and multi-faith neighbourhood. Nearly 30 per cent of students were of south Asian ethnicity, 12 per cent black, and fewer than 50 per cent were Roman Catholic. The proportion of Catholics fell further, to under 30 per cent by 1992, when there were 900 students on the roll, and in 1995, after a long-drawn-out and vitriolic campaign to save it, the governors closed the college. It was eventually re-opened as a non-denominational campus of South Birmingham College.

St Paul's High School for girls in Vernon Road was built to provide Catholic secondary education for girls in the city. It was opened in 1908 in a purpose-built, characteristically Edwardian building designed by Mr Sandy and funded by the Sisters of Charity of St Paul in Selly Park. It cost some £20,000. Teaching staff and all the head mistresses were drawn from the Order. There was inevitably a close relationship with the Oratory nearby and one of the brothers trained the school choir, which had an excellent reputation in the inter-war period. Like St Philip's it was evacuated to

136 St Paul's High School, *c.*1930: the 'Wrenaissance' main school building was opened in 1910.

137 The housecraft room at St Paul's.

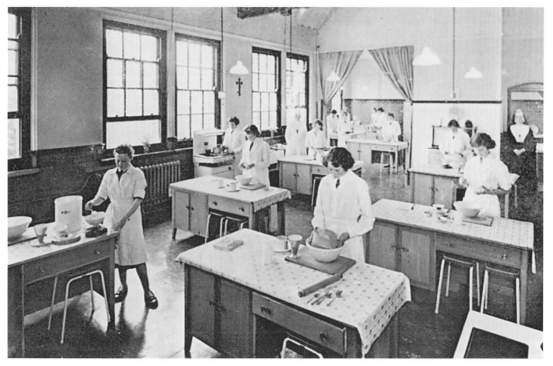

Hereford in 1939. The High School began sixth-form teaching in 1922 and had become three-form entry by 1954. It became a direct grant school after the Second World War, then a Voluntary Aided school, and finally a comprehensive school in 1975, losing the 'High' from its name. New buildings were added to the site in 1966 but the block was destroyed by fire in 1973. It was not until 1977 that work began on replacement buildings. In modern times Clare Short, Minister for Overseas Development and MP for Ladywood constituency, is perhaps the school's most famous old girl.

Edgbaston Church of England College for Girls

This school occupied a fine Georgian house on Calthorpe Road and was founded in 1886 by a group of clergymen which included Dr Charles Gore, the Bishop of Worcester, and later first Bishop of Birmingham. They were concerned that many of the girls schools in the city had too secular an outlook. The school has since been substantially extended, though the original house remains, as do the park-like grounds to the rear. The Anglican tradition of the school has been maintained to the present thanks to good relationships with St George's Church opposite, but in 1999, in common with an increasing number of independent schools, the school became co-educational and changed its name to St George's School.

Edgbaston High School for Girls

This school was formed in 1876 and is particularly associated with the education reformer George Dixon. Having made his fortune at a comparatively young age, like many of his contemporaries he became a city councillor in 1863, was mayor in 1867, and in the same year was elected MP for Edgbaston North. He resigned his seat in 1876 because of his wife's ill health. He was not one of the Unitarian or Quaker families who dominated mid-Victorian Birmingham society and politics. He was an Anglican, his passion was education, and he

believed it was the function of the state and not the Church. He founded the National Education League, again in 1867, to campaign for a free, compulsory, non-sectarian state education system for all children between the ages of five and thirteen.

In 1876 Dixon convened a meeting at his house in Edgbaston by sending out invitations to 52 local families to discuss founding a non-denominational girls high school. Twenty-two sent representatives. At the time there was no high school for girls in Birmingham and Dixon had three daughters amongst his six children. His idea was to ask the Girls Public Day School Co. Ltd in London to found a school, for which they required suitable premises and local subscriptions for 400 £5 shares. Shareholders could then nominate their own children as pupils and could nominate others at fees of between two and five guineas per term. The meeting adopted the scheme almost entirely but decided they did not want the involvement of a London-based company; they had more than enough business experience between them to run the school themselves! The original committee of 15 included no fewer than six women, at a time when it was very unusual to find women participating in public affairs.

The initial proposal for premises was to combine with the Birmingham and Edgbaston Proprietary School for boys at Five Ways and convert the headmaster's house there for the girls. However, this proved unsuitable and a separate school was decided upon. With an advance of £2,000 from Sir Josiah Mason towards the total cost of £3,500, they purchased the lease of the house which stood at the junction of Hagley and Harborne Roads at Five Ways. A company was formed with 243 shares of £10 each and a governing body was established, with Dixon as first chairman, of which it was agreed at least one-third had to be women. By late summer Miss Alice Cooper had been appointed headmistress. She came from London, but was a Unitarian and so

138 Church of England School for Girls, 1898: like most private schools in Edgbaston, the CESG occupied a number of former private mansions.

139 Girls and staff at the Church of England School: unfortunately this is undated.

slipped easily into Edgbaston society. By the end of the year the house was ready and 76 girls were enrolled into four classes. Miss Cooper was a great advocate of science for girls, which would certainly have been attractive to Birmingham's industrial élite, though to begin with there was no laboratory in the school. But then there was no library either! Regular lessons occupied only the mornings; the afternoons were taken up with 'extras'.

In 1878 the school council bought 'The Laurels', a lovely Adam-stye house next door, since the number of pupils had doubled. Its garden enabled the girls to participate in games, for which the 'garden club' was formed, and cricket, tennis, rounders and badminton were all played, though with some difficulty since there was a large tree in the middle of the lawn! Miss Cooper invited C.L. Dodgson (Lewis Carroll) to the school in 1889 to see a

performance of 'Alice in Wonderland', and after the performance he was persuaded to tell the story of 'Bruno's Picnic' to the audience from the stage. The school continued to increase in size and, as it did so, so did its catchment area. In 1893 the school council arranged for a 'Moseley bus' to be provided, at a cost of 6d. per day, for girls from that growing suburb; a year or two later a second bus was required. They were superseded in 1913 when a public bus service began between Moseley and Five Ways. A boarding house was added in the 1890s and a preparatory department for young girls in 1913.

It was the preparatory department which was the cause of a major crisis in 1924 when its teacher, Miss Woodhall, claimed that it was a separate school and refused to carry out the wishes of the headmistress, Miss Young. The council prevaricated and Miss Young resigned,

140   The George Dixon Schools in City Road soon after completion in 1906.

together with 10 of her staff, and many parents took their daughters away since Miss Young was a popular teacher. Her successor, Miss Elsie Collier, brought 10 new teachers with her from Windsor and the council learnt their lesson, establishing firmly that the preparatory school was under the headship of the senior school. However, it was a decade before the school recovered its equilibrium, and financial crises continued to plague it for thirty years.

The school was evacuated to Stroud High School for Girls at the start of the Second World War but, as with most evacuated schools, was back in Birmingham by January 1940. The end of the war brought a new crisis since the Calthorpe leases expired in 1946. A five-year extension was granted but the estate was aware that the school site was going to be commercially valuable in the coming decades and suggested the school move elsewhere. However,

the council decided it was unable to finance a complete new school building and persuaded the Calthorpe estate to grant a 40-year lease on the existing premises. They also purchased the leases of adjoining houses in Hagley Road since, by 1950, there were over 600 pupils in the school. The 1958 city plan scheduled the school site for high-rise office development and this meant an enormous increase in its potential value. Consequently, in 1960, the school, in conjunction with the Calthorpe estate, agreed to move to a new site in Westbourne Road. This provided room for extensive playing fields and new buildings designed by Maurice Hobbiss and it moved in 1963. A swimming pool, used by the other schools nearby, was added in 1965 and the school has enjoyed a long period of enhanced reputation since then, so that the buildings were substantially extended in the 1990s.

Local Authority Secondary Schools

George Dixon Boys and Girls County Grammar Schools were opened in 1906 in new purpose-built buildings on City Road as a replacement for the higher grade schools in Oozells Street. They were amongst the first state grammar schools in the city. It took a number of years before the majority of pupils completed the five-year course and, although fees were charged until 1938, most pupils progressed to George Dixon from local state elementary schools. The girls school was damaged by a land mine in the Second World War, which fell on houses opposite. The school's claim to TV fame is that Michael Balcon, the film producer and deviser of the PC George Dixon character, was an old boy. Stanmore Road Secondary Modern School was built on the playing fields of George Dixon to cater for the post-war baby boom in the late 1950s, but it was combined with the older school when George Dixon became a comprehensive school in 1973.

Harborne Hill County Secondary School was opened in 1952. Together with the Lordswood grammar-technical schools, and Stanmore and Portland Road secondary schools, it was part of a planned and co-ordinated scheme on the part of the local education authority to provide replacements for old-fashioned and bomb-damaged schools in the inner-ring housing areas, and to cater for the post-war baby boom. The design of Harborne Hill had an overtly political motive. Attlee's Labour government wanted to demonstrate that a well-equipped and well-designed secondary modern school, able to enter pupils for the new GCE examinations, could offer an education comparable with the traditional grammar schools and thereby gain popular approval for education reform. The GCE examinations, unlike the preceding Matriculation, could be examined in individual subjects, and these were greatly extended to include a wide variety of practical subjects. Facilities for these practical subjects were a special feature of Harborne Hill. The teaching accommodation is arranged

round a quadrangle and includes rooms for woodwork, metalwork, art, technical drawing, needlework and domestic science (including a fully furnished flat with en suite bathroom for teaching housecraft). The assembly hall, opening directly from the entrance hall, with its impressive portico, could seat 600 and has a ciné projection room and a stage with a scenery fly tower. The steel-framed building, clad with brick, needed extensive repair in the 1990s as the steel had corroded. At the same time unsightly later extensions were removed and the laboratories and practical rooms were refurbished.

Another new feature of Harborne Hill was the provision for adult education with its own entrance and administrative area. Classes included both academic subjects at GCE, practical subjects such as car maintenance and cookery, and recreational subjects such as yoga and wine tasting. There was a particularly popular class in coastal navigation; Brummies have always been keen on the sea since they are as far from it as it is possible to be in Britain! There were over 1,000 adults a week attending in the mid-1980s but then political change forced adult classes to be self-funding and increased fees forced most classes to close.

The Lordswood Schools were technical grammar schools when they were founded in the far corner of Edgbaston parish near to Bearwood and therefore of a higher status than Harborne Hill. They too were intended to draw in a wider cross-section of children than the King Edward's Grammar Schools by offering the broad range of technical and practical subjects already described for Harborne Hill but with high-quality teaching of academic subjects as well, offered to advanced level in the sixth form.

The problem for all these schools from the 1970s was their location. Edgbaston had been a good place to build schools because it offered extensive sites for modern school buildings and playing fields, under the control of a single landowner with whom the local

141 'Hallfield' now occupied by Priory School.

142 West House School was founded in this house in 1895.

143 Lawrence Levy, founder of Birmingham Jewish Collegiate School.

authority could negotiate easily. Unfortunately, there were relatively few children of secondary age in their catchment areas to begin with, and this problem got worse from the 1970s onwards as the post-war generation reached adulthood. Lordswood fared best as its sixth form meant that it had a good academic and pastoral reputation. Harborne Hill also survives, though it was threatened with closure several times. Stanmore and Portland Road were eventually closed and provision in north Edgbaston was concentrated at George Dixon School.

Preparatory Schools

There were a large number of preparatory schools in Edgbaston in the 19th century, most of which catered for pupils to the age of 14, and few of which have survived to the present. Some were faith-based and were affected by the provision of both the denominational

grammar schools and King Edward's, Five Ways after 1880, which has already been described. Thus, 'Penryn', in Somerset Road, was an independent Catholic school for boys which was based in what was originally a private residence designed in Victorian Gothic style by J.H. Chamberlain. It operated successfully into the middle of the 20th century. It was matched, from 1936, by the Convent of the Holy Child Jesus School, located in 'Hallfield' at the top of Priory Road, which provided for girls. This school still survives, though it has recently changed its name to 'Priory School', become co-educational, and caters for the full age range from nursery to eighteen.

'Hallfield' had been built as a private house in the late 1830s but was remodelled in 1890 by the architectural firm of Chamberlain and Martin for Edward Nettlefold. It was adapted for Hallfield Preparatory School in 1910 after Mrs Nettlefold's death. Hallfield moved to 'Southfield' in Church Road in 1936, became 'Edgbaston Preparatory School, Hallfield', flourished, purchased 'Beech Lawn', next door, in 1968 and continues to thrive there with many new buildings. In a similar way, West House Preparatory School in St James's Road was founded in the house of that name in 1895, taking over 'Woodbourne' soon afterwards, and Wilton House in the 1960s. It, too, continues to flourish. These last two schools were non-denominational.

More distinctive was the Birmingham Jewish Collegiate School, founded in 1875 by Lawrence Levy at his home, No. 75 Wheeley's Road. Levy had begun as assistant master at the Hebrew Schools in Singers Hill but supplemented his meagre salary with private tuition. His success encouraged him to establish his own school, which succeeded in gaining more scholarships for King Edward's School than any other contemporary private school. However, it closed in 1891 because of the competition from KES, Five Ways, 17 of his pupils moving there in its first year. Levy's memoirs mention other small competing private schools such as

144 Children from the Bluecoat School enjoying the gardens of the new site in August 1913. This delightful photograph is by Sir Benjamin Stone.

145 The neo-Georgian buildings of the Bluecoat School opened in 1930.

146   The Walker Hall in Ampton Road originates from 1847, when the two buildings were the boys and girls Church of England elementary schools.

Slack's School, in Carpenter Road, run by the Rev. John Slack, a prominent nonconformist clergyman, and Harris's School in Gough Road, where 'the school fights between my school and Harris's were very real things. Harris's completely besieged us one afternoon!'

Elementary Education

Like King Edward's, the Blue Coat School was originally located in the city centre in St Philip's churchyard (Birmingham Cathedral), where it was built in 1724 to provide for the elementary education of 150 boys and 100 girls, 'teaching them to read and write, and instructing them in the knowledge of the Christian religion'. It was, of course, a charity school, not the private preparatory school it has since become. In the early 20th century it was recognised that the city centre was not an appropriate location for the school and it was proposed to relocate to the suburb of Olton, building a new school on land which the school governors had acquired.

Finance was to come from the sale of the city centre site. An architectural competition was held for the design of the new school, most entrants to which pointed out the unsuitability of the new site for a school. Consequently the governors began again, this time negotiating with the Calthorpe estate. In 1913 Harborne Hill House, a rambling mansion in 17 acres of grounds on what had been part of Harborne Heath (though in Edgbaston parish), was purchased for £7,500 (a low price 'fixed with the desire of assisting the school') to provide a site for a new school building. The prominent Birmingham Arts and Crafts architect, J.L. Ball, provided the winning design in a quiet neo-Georgian style, but the outbreak of the First World War, and then the Depression, meant that plans had to be delayed. Meanwhile, the estate was used for growing vegetables to improve the diet of the children in the city centre, and as a sports field. A pavilion and changing room was provided in 1924.

The city centre site was finally purchased by Birmingham City Council in 1927, releasing finance; Ball's designs for the new school were revised by H.W. Simister, and work started in 1929. The new school opened in October 1930. It was built as five houses, three for boys and two for girls, arranged around three sides of a grassy quadrangle. It reflects the more homely domestic ideals that had been used for the design of children's homes since the late 19th century. There was also a large chapel. The pupils continued to wear their distinctive 18th-century blue uniforms right up until the transfer to Edgbaston. The sculptured figures of a boy and girl pupil in the original uniforms, which had been placed over the door of the city centre school in 1770, were taken to the new school but are kept inside; replicas stand in the niche outside. The school became a local authority Voluntary Aided primary school in 1948 and the education authority purchased seven acres of the site adjoining Harborne Road for Harborne Hill School. The new arrangements did not last for long, and by 1952 the trustees had decided to convert the school into an independent boarding and day preparatory school for 200 pupils. Inevitably this proved controversial, but the charitable intent of the founders was safeguarded by providing 30 'foundation scholarships'. This new structure came into being in 1956, though it was not completed until 1960. The sale of part of the charity estate in Sparkbrook raised £2 million for endowments and building improvements, and the sale, in 1980, of the remaining 2.4 acres of the school site fronting Harborne Road for housing and a new municipal library provided further funds for new classrooms and the science, art and library building, opened in 1989. Meanwhile, the chapel was graced by a large 1908 organ obtained from St Wulstan's church, Bournbrook.

Elementary education in Edgbaston was provided by the churches in the mid-19th century. We have seen that St Bartholomew's had a school house beside the churchyard from the 16th century at least, but in 1847 the new Edgbaston C. of E. school was provided in Ampton Road, financed from subscriptions in the parish. There were both boys and girls departments from the beginning, with about 200 pupils in total. When it closed in 1934, the school was used by St James's C. of E. School until 1940. During the war the building was used as a British Restaurant, providing wholesome meals at lunchtime for those who worked in the parish. After the war it was converted into a church hall and thanks to a trust fund provided by Miss Walker, after whom it was renamed, is maintained to the highest standards and used frequently by local schools for examinations, and as the headquarters of Moseley Bridge Club.

St George's Vestry decided in 1852 that the growing population of the parish demanded a new school. Lord Calthorpe offered a site in Beaufort Road on the corner with Plough and Harrow Road and by 1854 the school was ready for occupation. It consisted of a schoolroom (accommodating 165!) and teacher's house; pupils were charged 2d. a week. Two pupil-teachers and a monitor helped Miss Healey, the mistress, to organise lessons. This first classroom was for girls and infants; a boys schoolroom was not added until 1870. In 1930-1 it was reorganised into a Junior and Infant School. A completely new building was opened in 1968 and the school continues its work in what is now urban priority area conditions. St James's C. of E. School occupied a site between Gough Road and Summer Road and was opened in 1861 for 300 pupils, both boys and girls. It was enlarged and adapted several times in the 1920s and '30s but was then damaged by enemy action in 1941 and closed. Finally, George Dixon County Primary School, in City Road, was a large mixed infant school for 600 pupils located beside the new County Grammar School. It was reorganised in 1932 as a Junior and Infants school.

147   The Royal Institution for the Instruction of the Deaf and Dumb was founded in 1812.

Special Schools

The Royal Institution for the Instruction of Deaf and Dumb Children, in Church Road, was an institution of national renown. It was founded in 1812 by a physician at the General Hospital, Gabriel Jean Marie De Lys, who had been born in St Malo, Brittany but was a refugee from the terrors of the French Revolution. The school opened in 1814 and the core of the present buildings dates from the 1850s. It was enlarged and improved in 1887, again in 1897, and further in 1903-5. It provided education for 183 children originally and continued operating until 1984. In that year it was renamed the Princess Royal Centre of the National Deaf-Blind and Rubella Association. Staff at the school were responsible for a number of important innovations in teaching deaf children,

including a typing system of embossed short-hand to make reading easier and quicker. De Lys died in 1831 and is one of the few people accorded a memorial tablet in the parish church.

Almost next door, though across the railway and canal, and officially on Carpenter Road, was the Royal Institution for the Blind. This occupied a purpose-built building in the Jacobean style designed by Samuel Hemming in 1851-2. The school expanded rapidly, having 600 pupils a year by the turn of the century. It consequently outgrew its premises and moved to Lickey Grange, the former home of Lord Austin. The Edgbaston building became the headquarters of BBC Midlands in 1953 until their move to the new purpose-built studios at Pebble Mill in the late 1960s.

Fourteen

Sport and Recreation

The first sports club of which we have any record is bowls. A bowling green was established in Edgbaston in 1825, 'supported by a select body of subscribers'. Its half-acre grounds, containing bowling greens, a quoits ground, a 'commodious' cottage for the caretaker and surrounded by gardens 'tastefully planted with trees and shrubs', are recorded on Piggot-Smith's 1824-5 map in the north-west angle of Highfield Road and Harborne Road. The club was relocated into the middle of the street block by the Calthorpe's agent in the 1850s as its road frontages had become valuable. Its new site was so hidden that correspondents to *Edgbastonia* in 1882 were seemingly unaware of

its presence and could report only that it 'was never well supported'. However, it is still there, with its greens well-cared-for and its members still playing regularly.

Archery was the second sporting activity of which we have record, the Edgbaston Archery and Lawn Tennis Club continuing to occupy the valley bottom meadows of the Chad Brook below the Botanical Gardens. The second sport became by far the most significant by the later 19th century. The rifle range associated with the *Gun Barrels* public house on the Bournbrook boundary was another late 19th-century activity, and there is, too, a long established bowling club beside the pub.

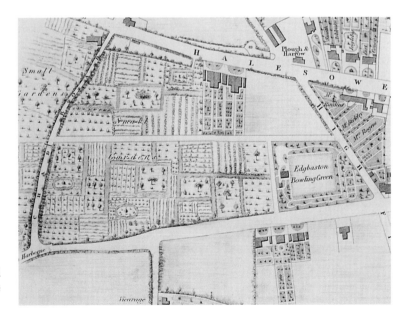

148 The Bowling Green and guinea gardens on Harborne Road, 1824-5.

149 'Fairlight', Ampton Road, where lawn tennis was invented.

150 Major T.H. Gem: Gem was a sports enthusiast and, with J.B.A. Perera, devised the game of lawn tennis in Edgbaston.

Lawn Tennis

Lawn tennis, it is claimed, was invented in Edgbaston, and there is a 'blue plaque' on a house in Ampton Road to prove it! The two men honoured are Major Thomas 'Harry' Gem and Mr J.B.A. Perera. Gem was the son of a Birmingham solicitor and a very active sportsman, playing cricket and rackets and participating in athletics and horse-riding. At the age of 43 he ran the 21 miles from Birmingham to Warwick in a little over three hours! Rackets required an expensively constructed court and the aim of his new game was to get much of the excitement of rackets but on a level lawn. With his friend Perera, a Great Charles Street merchant, he devised the rules for a game which they first called 'pelota' but subsequently renamed 'lawn rackets', and the first experimental match took place on Perera's lawn, at 'Fairlight', in Ampton Road, in 1866. Both men subsequently moved to Leamington Spa and there established the first club for their game, codifying the rules and changing its name once more to 'lawn tennis'.

By the 1890s no respectable house in Edgbaston was without its tennis lawn and a number of clubs were formed. Priory Lawn Tennis Club dates from 1875, Edgbaston Lawn Tennis Club from 1878, and Edgbaston Archery and Lawn Tennis Club from 1881. By 1882 a Midland Counties Tournament was held at the Edgbaston club's ground in Edgbaston Park Road. Both clubs produced Wimbledon winners in those far-off days when English players could do such things! However, probably the best courts in Edgbaston were those at Tally Ho!, beside the River Rea, on the site of Edgbaston Mill. In 1927 an England v Sweden European Zone Davis Cup match was played here, England winning 4-1. Additional tennis facilities were provided by many of Edgbaston's institutions, such as the university and the schools, and a few manufacturing firms. By the 1950s there were 10 clubs affiliated to the Warwickshire Lawn Tennis Association, whilst in the 1930s the Edgbaston and Priory clubs

151 A match in progress at Priory Tennis Club in 1937: Dorothy Round is playing Senorita Lizana.

were active supporters of squash too, and squash courts were added to their facilities.

The most famous recent player belonging to these clubs is Ann Jones (formerly Miss A.S. Haydon) who was Wimbledon Women's Singles and Mixed Doubles Champion in 1969, and captain of the British Wightman Cup Team in 1971-2. Her 1969 Singles win was against Billie-Jean King and she had also been losing finalist in 1967. Remarkably, she had also been a women's table-tennis international in the 1954-9 period.

In the later 20th century all the Edgbaston clubs had difficulties because their land became susceptible to urban development as leases needed to be renewed. This is what happened to the Tally Ho! Club. The site is now derelict but subject to controversial development proposals by the Calthorpe estate. In 1964 a fire destroyed Priory's clubhouse and Priory and Edgbaston decided to merge to form a stronger organisation on a commercial basis. Edgbaston's courts were sold to the University of Birmingham for student residences and Priory was developed with modern facilities. Courts include indoor, lawn, artificial lawn, clay and all-weather surfaces and several courts are floodlit. Facilities were of sufficiently high standard for the club to host the Dow (now DFS) Classic Ladies Tournament from 1982, which is an important pre-Wimbledon tournament with all the world's top players competing. Equally significant are the squash facilities, the 10 courts having viewing galleries and three being glass-backed. Consequently the club has hosted the British Open Championships.

152 Edgbaston Hall became the golf club clubhouse in 1936.

The Golf Course

Edgbaston Golf Club was formed in 1896, soon after other clubs had been formed in Moseley and Harborne. Its first course of nine holes was in Warley Park and there were 37 initial members, including 14 women; play was limited to weekdays at first but this was quickly changed. In 1907 Birmingham Corporation proposed to make a new public park of the Warley estate and so the club sought a new home. By 1910 the club had agreed to lease some 84 acres of Tennal Hall Farm in Harborne for 21 years. A full 18-hole course and new clubhouse were constructed within a year and by 1911 the club had 166 members. In the early 1930s the club's finances were in a bad way and it almost went into voluntary liquidation. However, this period also saw the first negotiations with the Calthorpe estate, who were themselves proposing to turn the park and hall into a golf club. The hall had not been lived in since it had been vacated by Sir James Smith, Birmingham's first lord mayor, who had lived there from 1908 to 1932. The problem was that the park was too small for 18 holes and it was only in 1936 when additional land at 'Park Mount' became available, to the south, for holes three to six that the decision was taken to move the club from Harborne to Edgbaston. The trustees of the Calthorpe estate offered the club a loan to construct the course

and convert the hall to a clubhouse, together with a 50-year lease. In 1936-7 the park was laid out as a golf course by H.S. Colt, of Colt, Allison and Harrison. Besides the planting of a large number of silver birch trees, and the felling of nearly 400 other trees, the design required the lake to be lowered so as to make room for the 13th fairway, thereby making the brick dam more visible and leading to a massive infestation of flies and midges in the first season. Other areas of the course required building up and earth was acquired from the site of the KES swimming pool and from the Five Ways underpass. More recently the old kitchen garden has been largely destroyed for car parks, practice greens and a helicopter landing pad! The course must be closer to a major city centre than any other in Britain, but remains remarkably tranquil and rural in outlook.

Warwickshire Cricket

There were a very large number of cricket clubs in Birmingham by the later 19th century. The Ordnance Survey map shows club grounds in Edgbaston opposite 'The Elms' in Edgbaston Park Road, in Edward Road, opposite Calthorpe Park, and, of course, the county cricket ground on Edgbaston Road. To those not resident in Birmingham 'Edgbaston' means the Warwickshire county ground and its current test match status means that the name is known in all those parts of the world where cricket is played. The Warwickshire club has its origins in a meeting organised in March 1882, in Leamington Spa, by the Warwickshire Gentleman's Club, at which there was general agreement that a broadly-based county club should be formed; some weeks later, at another meeting in Coventry, the new club was founded. There were several years of discussion before it was accepted that economics determined that the club's ground had to be in Birmingham and, in 1885, the club took a 21-year lease on 12 acres of meadowland beside the River Rea offered by the Calthorpe estate. It was estimated that enclosing and draining the ground and building a pavilion would cost some £1,250 and so a company was formed, with a capital of £3,000 in £10 shares, to lease the ground to the club. The first match there took place on 7 June 1886, in front of 3,000 spectators, against the MCC. It was abandoned as a draw so as to allow the MCC players to catch the train back to London. Warwickshire was captained by G.H. Cartland of Kings Heath, who was to become chairman of the club for 46 years! In August the Australian team came to play their first match against Warwickshire but only one day's play was possible because of rain.

Like most sports clubs, Warwickshire CCC's history is part dominated by the exploits of its teams and individuals and part by the administrative abilities of its secretaries and committee. Warwickshire's first secretary was William Ansell and he was determined to get the team into the County Championship. That meant some professional players and ground improvements. Warwickshire was admitted to the Championship in 1893, midway through the season. The 20 years after 1890 were marked by a large number of drawn matches because of the beautiful wickets prepared by the first groundsman, John Bates. These included a match in 1896 which produced a record county innings (which still stands today) of 887 runs by the Yorkshire team. In 1911 the captaincy of the club was offered to 22-year-old F.R. Foster, a pace bowler and mid-order batsman. In his first season he topped both the batting and bowling averages and Warwickshire became county champions for the first time. Foster was injured in a wartime road accident and could not resume playing in 1919.

153   Warwickshire County Cricket Club's first pavilion, *c.*1895.

154   Painting from the pavilion of a match in progress, *c.*1895.

Edgbaston's first test match, against the Australian side, was in 1902, by which time, thanks to embankments constructed by the corporation, the ground could accommodate more than 20,000 spectators. On the first day England declared at 376 for nine and then bowled Australia out for 36 runs! Then it rained, and rained, leaving the pitch a lake. Only two more tests were played at Edgbaston before the Second World War since ground improvements were required. In 1919 the club purchased the freehold of the ground, together with another six acres of adjoining land fronting Pershore Road, which had been used by Birmingham Rugby Club. There were plans for seating stands, terracing and a new pavilion but little money to pay the £200,000 estimated cost. Inter-war teams did not help with the consistent mediocrity of their play.

Change came after the Second World War. H.E. 'Tom' Dollery became the club's first professional captain in 1949 and, with a squad of only 13 players, all but one of them professionals, Warwickshire were county champions again in 1951. One commentator suggested that they were 'an extraordinary team of ordinary players'. Meanwhile Leslie Deakins, the new club secretary, set about improving the ground. Finance came from a football pool which the committee considered 'an undignified

method of obtaining funds'. However, it could not be ignored, and from 1953 the Warwickshire Supporters' Club football pool grew to become the most successful in the country. By 1972 it had raised more than £2 million for cricket in Warwickshire, including £1 million to transform the Edgbaston ground into one of the best in the country. Consequently test cricket returned to Birmingham in 1957 and has continued each summer since. The arrival of Dennis Amiss in 1958 marked the beginning of another phase of improvement for the team. By the time he retired in 1987 he had scored more runs and more centuries for his county than any other player and been capped for England 50 times. Warwickshire were runners-up in the Championship in 1971 and Champions once more in 1972.

The mid-1990s were golden years for Warwickshire. They were county champions in 1994 and 1995 and became the only team ever to win three of the four domestic trophies in 1994. 1995 was also the season in which West Indian batsman Brian Lara scored a world record innings of 501, against Durham at Edgbaston. 2002 has seen the construction of new stands on the River Rea side of the ground and centenary celebrations of Test cricket at Edgbaston.

Chapter Fifteen

Post-War Development

Three themes dominate the decade following the Second World War. First, many of the original leases on the great Victorian houses at the core of the Calthorpe estate were coming to an end and either required renewal or decisions to be taken on redevelopment; whilst there was indecision and uncertainty, property prices fell, some houses were left empty and began to fall into dereliction, and others were subdivided into flats or used for professional consulting rooms or offices. Secondly, most of the larger houses had been built to be run by servants in an age of cheap coal. By the 1950s there were neither servants nor cheap fuel! Professional families now began to look to the newer, smaller, more fuel-efficient, executive family homes being built in Solihull and Sutton Coldfield, rather than the grand houses of Edgbaston. Thirdly, the city council in the new 'age of planning' began to cast envious eyes on the empty green spaces and low-density houses of Edgbaston as a place where new homes could be built for families displaced by slum clearance under way in Birmingham's over-crowded zone of back-to-back courtyard houses.

The forward-thinking reaction of the Calthorpe estate was to commission their own professional 'town-plan' from local architect John Madin to set the framework for redevelopment and refurbishment over the remainder of the 20th century. The plan, which was published in 1958, is thought to be the first such commission by a private urban estate anywhere in Britain. It was put into effect immediately as a development framework, since Madin had taken the precaution of working closely with the city planning department. That it was effective was due to the leasehold control of properties by the Calthorpe estate. Effectively, they were able to use the falling in of leases to assemble large areas for redevelopment in the same way as local authorities could use compulsory purchase orders. This meant that new developments were large-scale, in harmonious architectural styles, preserved trees and enhanced landscaping, and provided effective new road networks and footpaths 'winding their way among the trees to the existing road system', as the plan somewhat picturesquely put it.

Madin's plan for the new Edgbaston was carefully conceived. It provided the higher densities that the city council required, through carefully sited developments of tower blocks and three-storey slab blocks of flats, together with garage blocks, set in designed landscapes which preserved as many of the mature trees as possible. It sold land on the edges of the estate to the city council, for their own development of flats and houses, with encouragement to preserve trees and shrubberies in these areas too. Two small local shopping centres were also planned to provide social amenities for the eastern and western parts of the estate respectively. The *quid pro quo* was that the Calthorpe estate gained planning consent for the redevelopment of the Five Ways area for office and business development. Finally, the core of the estate was preserved for single-family

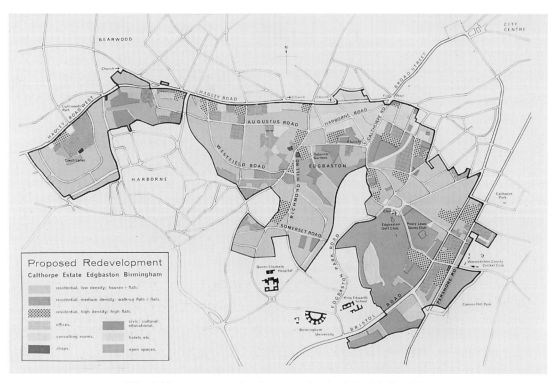

155 Calthorpe estate redevelopment plan by John Madin, 1958.

156 'Footpaths winding their way among the trees', Harborne Road.

housing in new estates of detached dwellings around culs-de-sac. By 1971 the density of population on the estate was up to 30 persons per acre, and the population had risen from 8,000 to 26,000.

Some of the earliest of these new developments were the High Point flats in Richmond Hill Road and the commercial developments near Five Ways. Amongst the earliest new office buildings, with characteristic glazed walls, were the Chamber of Commerce building at the junction of Harborne Road and Highfield Road, designed by Madin himself; Shell-BP House on Calthorpe Road; and the Midland

Employer's Mutual Assurance Building on Hagley Road. By 1965 Auchinleck House, with its 10 floors of offices, 60 shops and 'first-class restaurant', was being 'topped out' by Lord Mayor, Alderman Fred Price, who happened to be Deputy Managing Director of Murrayfield Real Estate Co., the developers. By common consent this was, architecturally, one of Birmingham's best modern office buildings and, with its well-maintained modern light sculptures and prominent site, was seen by thousands of commuters into Birmingham each day. Many were outraged when a recent refurbishment banished the sculptures in favour of grey panels and meaningless paint squiggles.

Three years later the Edgbaston Shopping Centre was built on the former site of Edgbaston High School for Girls, opposite Auchinleck House, between Harborne and Hagley Roads, and to the rear of what was then the headquarters of Tube Investments (TI). The Centre had a 17-storey office tower, 34 shops, a 10,000 sq. ft. supermarket, a large restaurant, and parking for 250 cars on the roof. It was designed by T.P. Bennett & Sons of London and built by Bernard Sunley & Sons. Office development has continued at Five Ways and along the Hagley Road so that this has become one of the principal centres of high office towers in the city. More recently, the development of Broad Street as a restaurant and entertainments complex, following the building of the International Convention Centre, has begun to spill over into Hagley Road. The large mansions beyond the office quarter began conversion into hotels in the 1960s, and a number of purpose-built hotels were also constructed. This trend has accelerated in recent years as demand for high quality hotel space has increased exponentially. The Tube Investments HQ building at Five Ways is especially notable for its conversion to the city's only 'five star' hotel (now the Birmingham Marriott), which was used for President Clinton's visit to Birmingham for the G8 summit in 1998.

157 Local authority housing, Pershore Road.

158 'High Point' by John Madin, Richmond Hill Road.

159 Chamber of Commerce building by John Madin, soon after completion c.1960.

160 No. 54 Hagley Road: this office block was designed by John Madin Design Group and completed in 1976-7.

Madin's plan was about redevelopment, but by the 1960s some were equally concerned to preserve the best of the old. As early as 1958 the Georgian Society had prepared a list of houses they deemed worthy of preservation and in 1961 the Victorian Society proposed a conservation area and some 61 buildings for statutory listing. A decade later little had happened except that eight of the 29 buildings listed had been demolished! In 1972 the Calthorpe estate commissioned Donald Insall & Associates to draw up a conservation plan for the estate. This, too, was remarkably conservative, suggesting only a number of small conservation areas in the eastern part of the estate and saying little about the west. Even by the middle 1970s, therefore, the development and conservation policies within the Calthorpe estate were combining to preserve some of the earliest houses, which were more suitable for refurbishing for either modern homes or offices, whilst demolishing the larger and more spectacular mid- and late 19th-century mansions, which were not easily converted.

A decade later the city council had begun to appreciate the benefits of conservation and there was a new appreciation of the city's heritage of fine Arts and Crafts houses. Five Conservation Areas were declared in Edgbaston, four of them small and very specific, one very large and enclosing almost the whole of the eastern half of the Calthorpe estate. The distinctive late-Georgian/Regency terraces in Lee Crescent and Ryland Road became separate but adjoining Conservation Areas; the circus of late-Victorian houses around St Augustine's Church, and the houses designed by Arts and Crafts architect J.L. Ball in Barnsley Road, both on the Gillott estate of north Edgbaston, became distinct Conservation Areas; whilst almost the whole area bounded by Hagley Road to the north, Lee Bank Middleway to the east, Bristol Road to the south, and Edgbaston Park Road, Pritchatts Road and Richmond Hill Road to the west was designated as Edgbaston Conservation Area. Within this

161 Tricorn House: this distinctive office building on the north side of Five Ways was built in 1975.

162 & 163 Lee Crescent: the conservation plan and restored buildings. This was Birmingham's contribution to European Architectural Heritage Year.

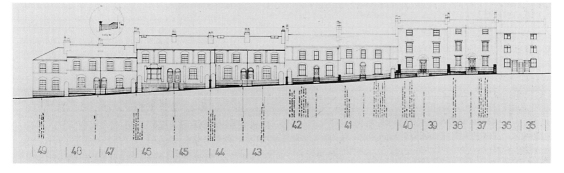

164 Steel Sculpture, Five Ways: art works were added to development schemes in the 1970s and this stainless steel tube sculpture was designed by Alexander Mann and constructed by TI Stainless Tubes Ltd in 1972.

165 The Five Ways clock, one of a number of such clocks added to the Birmingham street scene *c.*1900.

latter there are also four large areas designated as Parks and Gardens of Special Historic Interest (Edgbaston Park; The Vale; Birmingham Botanical Garden; and Westbourne Road Leisure Gardens), a Nature Reserve (Edgbaston Park beech woods) and a Site of Special Scientific Interest (Spurrier's Pool). There are also more than 250 listed buildings.

Elsewhere in Edgbaston other developments were under way. The city council's comprehensive redevelopment proposals of the 1950s impinged on the boundaries of the suburb. To the north, the Ladywood estates of local authority housing occupy the area beyond Duchess and Beaufort Roads. To the east, the area below St James's Church has become a local authority estate with new primary school and Birmingham's first drive-through McDonald's restaurant. Most of the area of terraced housing to the north-east of Calthorpe Park has been rebuilt with modern homes, and the land between Pershore and Bristol Roads was redeveloped with tower blocks and maisonettes, most of the latter now having been replaced for the second time in 50 years. The three most spectacular new institutional buildings are probably the windowless Masonic Temple on the north side of Hagley Road, designed by John Madin and opened in 1972, and the new headquarters and studios of BBC Midlands at Pebble Mill, opened in the mid-1960s. Its popular midday magazine-news programme, 'Pebble Mill at One', brought Edgbaston's former mill site national fame. Thirdly, there is the Birmingham Police Training Centre on the Pershore Road, completed in 1960-4, which has social facilities, sports grounds, indoor riding school, stables and the Home Office Detective Training School. At the start of the 21st century Edgbaston remains a significant suburb where important decisions are made and things happen; university, hospitals, schools, BBC, and cricket periodically bring the place to national attention, but it is also a good place to live and work.

Bibliography

General Briggs, A., *History of Birmingham II Borough and City 1865-1938* (Oxford University Press, London, 1952)

Stephens, W.B. (ed.), *The Victoria History of Warwickshire VII. The City of Birmingham* (Oxford University Press, London, 1964)

Sutcliffe, A. and Smith, R., *Birmingham 1939-1970* (Oxford University Press, London, 1974)

One St Joseph, J.K. and Shotton, F.W., 'The Roman camps at Metchley, Birmingham', *Transactions, Birmingham Archaeological Society*, 58, 1934, pp.68-83

Webster, G., 'Further excavations at the Roman forts at Metchley, Birmingham, 1954', *Transactions, Birmingham Archaeological Society*, 72, 1954, pp.1-4

BUFAU, *The Romans in Birmingham. Metchley Roman Fort* (University of Birmingham, Birmingham, 2000)

Two Bassett, S., 'Anglo-Saxon Birmingham', *Midland History*, XXV, 2000, pp.1-28

Gover, J.E.B., Mawer, A. and Stenton, F.M., *The Place-Names of Warwickshire* (Cambridge University Press, Cambridge, 1936)

Morris, J. (ed.), *Domesday Book. Warwickshire* (Phillimore, Chichester, 1976)

Morris Jones, J., *Rotton Park and Round About* (manuscript, Birmingham Local Studies Library, 1968)

While, L.G., *Rotton Park. A History* (manuscript, Birmingham Local Studies Library, 1980)

Three Phillimore, W.P.W., *Some Account of the Family of Middlemore* (Phillimore, London, 1901)

Four Dugdale, W., *The Antiquities of Warwickshire Illustrated, Vol. 2* (2nd edn. by W. Thomas) (J. Osborn and T. Longman, London, 1730)

Peck, T.W. and Wilkinson, K.D., *William Withering of Birmingham* (John Wright & Sons, Bristol, 1950)

Five Cannadine, D., *Lords and Landlords. The Aristocracy and the Towns 1774-1967* (Leicester University Press, Leicester, 1980)

Crawford, A. (ed.), *By Hammer and Hand. The Arts and Crafts Movement in Birmingham* (Birmingham Museums and Art Gallery, Birmingham, 1984)

Six Ballard, P., '*An Oasis of Delight*': *The History of Birmingham Botanical Gardens* (Duckworth, London, 1983)

Ballard, P., 'A Small Country House' in *Birmingham: Winterbourne and its Gardens 1903-1995* (University of Birmingham, Birmingham, 1995)

Ballard, P., 'The Edgbaston Conservation Area. A Landscape Study for Birmingham City Council' (unpubl. Birmingham City Council, 1997)

Public Parks and Pleasure Grounds (City of Birmingham, Birmingham, 1892)

Seven Census ennumerator's returns, 1851-1891 (unpublished). Microfilm copies in Birmingham Local Studies Library

Lloyd, H., *The Quaker Lloyds in the Industrial Revolution* (Hutchinsons, London, 1975)

Redfern, J.B., 'Elite suburbians: early Victorian Edgbaston', *Local Historian*, 15, 1983, pp.259-71

Eight   Chatwin, P.B., 'Edgbaston', *Transactions, Birmingham Archaeological Society*, 39, 1913, pp.5-35

Harkness, J.C. and Pinkess, J.R.H., *St George's Church Edgbaston 1838-1998* (St George's PCC, Birmingham, 1998)

Martin, B., *John Henry Newman, his Life and Work* (Chatto & Windus, London, 1982)

Nine   Broadbridge, S.R., *The Birmingham Canal Navigations I 1768-1846* (David and Charles, Newton Abbot, 1974)

Christiansen, R., *A Regional History of the Railways of Great Britain 7: The West Midlands* (David and Charles, Newton Abbot, 1973)

Gray, P., Keeley, M. and Seale, J., *Midland Red. A History of the Company and its Vehicles up to 1940* (Transport Publishing Co., Glossop, 1978)

Hadfield, M., *The Canals of the West Midlands* (David and Charles, Newton Abbot, 1966)

Harvey, D., *A Nostalgic Look at Birmingham Transport 1933-53. Vol II the Southern Routes* (Silver Link Publishing, Peterborough, 1994)

Keeley, M., *Bus Operators: Midland Red* (Ian Allan Ltd., London, 1983)

Smith, D. and Harrison, D., *The Harborne Express* (Brewin Books, Studley, 1995)

Ten   Ives, E., Drummond, D. and Schwarz, L., *The First Civic University. Birmingham 1880-1980. An Introductory History* (University of Birmingham Press, Birmingham, 2000)

Eleven   Barnes, S., *The Birmingham Hospitals Centre* (Stanford and Mann, Birmingham, 1952)

Hall, D.L., *The Skin hospital Birmingham. A Century of Care 1881-1981* (West Birmingham Health District, Birmingham, 1981)

Jones, J.E., *A History of the Hospitals and other Charities of Birmingham* (Midland Educational Co. Ltd, Birmingham, n.d.)

Twelve   Candler, W.I., Jacques, A.M. and Dobbie, B.M.W., *King Edward VI High School for Girls Birmingham* (Ernest Benn Ltd, London, 1971)

Thomas, D., *The Edgbaston Preparatory School Hallfield, 1879-1994* (Edgbaston School, Birmingham, 1994)

Trott, A., *No Place for Fop or Idler. The Story of King Edward's School Birmingham* (James and James, London, 1992)

Thirteen   Levy, E.L., *Birmingham Jewry, 1870 Then, and 1929, Now* (Hammond, Birmingham, 1929)

Myhill, J.D., *Blue Coat. A History of the Blue Coat School, Birmingham 1772-1990* (Meridian Books, Warley, 1991)

Whitcut, J., *Edgbaston High School 1876-1976* (Edgbaston High School, Birmingham, 1976)

Worsley, M., *A History of St Philip's from Beginning to Beginning* (Wine Press, Tamworth, 1997)

Fourteen   Brooke, R. and Goodyear, D., *A Who's Who of Warwickshire County Cricket Club* (Robert Hale, London, 1989)

Duckworth, L., *The Story of Warwickshire Cricket 1882-1972* (Stanley Paul, London, 1974)

Heath, P., *Towards One Hundred Years. Edgbaston Golf Club 1896-1989* (Grant Books, Droitwich, 1986)

Fifteen   Insall & Associates, D.W., *Conservation in Edgbaston. A Report on the Calthorpe Estate* (London, 1973)

Pevsner, N. and Wedgwood, A., *The Buildings of England. Warwickshire* (Penguin Books, London, 1966)

Reilly, J.W., *Policing Birmingham. An Account of 150 Years of Police in Birmingham* (West Midlands Police, Birmingham, 1989)

Window on Edgbaston (Calthorpe Estate Office, Birmingham. n.d.)

Birmingham Newspaper Cuttings—Edgbaston June 1952-December 2000 (manuscript, Birmingham Local Studies Library, 2000)

Index

Page numbers in **bold** refer to illustrations or their captions